planning for the planet
dickenson
How Socialism Could Save the Environment

Planning for the Planet
How Socialism could save the Environment
Pete Dickenson
© Socialist Publications Ltd 2012

First Edition April 2012
Classification: Pete Dickenson
Environment/History/Politics/Economics

EAN-13: 978-1-870958-42-4

A catalogue record for this book is available from the British Library
Published by Socialist Publications
www.socialistworld.net
Typeset in Adobe Garamond Pro 10.5 pt
Printed by Russell Press (Nottingham)

Distribution by Socialist Books,
PO Box 24697, London, E11 1YD
Telephone +44 (0)20 8988 8789
e-mail: bookshop@socialistparty.org.uk
www.socialistbooks.co.uk

typesetting & design: dennis@kavitagraphics.co.uk

planning for the planet

pete dickenson

How Socialism Could Save the Environment

Published by Socialist Publications Ltd. March 2012

Contents

04	**Preface**
05	**Introduction**
09	Chapter 1: **The Planet in Danger**
10	1.1 The dangers of nuclear power
18	1.2 Toxic environmental contamination
20	1.3 Destruction of the natural world
22	Notes to Chapter 1
23	Chapter 2: **The Critical Threat of Global Warming**
25	2.1 Time rapidly running out to take action
32	2.2 The climate deniers
35	2.2.1 The arguments of the climate deniers
38	2.3 Decisive action needed now
30	Notes to Chapter 2.
41	Chapter 3: **How Green Will the Capitalists Go?**
42	3.1 Can market based approaches tackle global warming?
46	3.2 Constraints on capitalism
53	3.2.1 Direct state intervention
59	3.2.2 The lessons of the Copenhagen summit
65	3.3 The Green movement agenda
67	3.4 New Technology
70	3.5 The way forward
72	Appendix to Chapter 3. The Commoner-Erlich equations
	Notes to Chapter 3
73	Chapter 4: **A Socialist Programme for the Environment**
73	4.1 What needs to be done?
80	4.2 A socialist programme for the environment

82	4.2.1	Are there implications for living standards and jobs?
87	4.2.2	Summary of a socialist environmental programme
87		Notes to Chapter 4

89	**Chapter 5:**	**Planned Economy and the Environment**
89	5.1	Introduction
91	5.2	The elements of a planned economy
94	5.3	Planning techniques
97	5.3.1	Input-Output analysis
102	5.3.2	Planning for the environment
107		Appendix 1 to Chapter 5. The influence on Input-Output methods of Marx's theories of capital reproduction.
109		Appendix 2 to Chapter 5. A simple example demonstrating Input-Output methods.
114		Notes to Chapter 5

117	**Chapter 6:**	**In Defence of Socialist Planning**
117	6.1	Socialism and the limits to growth
123	6.2	Technical objections to planned economy
126	6.3	Lessons of the Soviet Union
134		Appendix to Chapter 6. The 'socialist calculation' controversy
		Notes to Chapter 6

139	**Chapter 7: A Warning to the Labour Movement**

145	**Bibliography**
149	**Index**

Preface

Twenty years have passed since the UN sponsored 'Earth Summit' in Rio de Janeiro highlighted the problem of global warming. In that time, output of greenhouse gases that cause climate change has escalated to a critical level that threatens environmental catastrophe. Since Rio, most socialists and radical Green activists have been extremely sceptical that meaningful action was being taken to address climate change. Now though, even those Greens who were prepared to be patient with the UN negotiations must surely be appalled at the total and abject failure of the main polluting countries to tackle global warming.

Ten years ago, in *Planning Green Growth*, I shared the deep scepticism of most on the Left that serious measures had been or would be taken to address environmental problems.[1] *Planning Green Growth* did not though rule out some new initiative, albeit inadequate and belated, since sections of the world's ruling classes realised something needed to be done. In the event, no policies were implemented to reduce even the rate of growth of greenhouse gas emissions, never mind to cut it. This book argues from a Marxist perspective that the failure to take action is a reflection of a deepening antagonism between the main capitalist powers, preventing any agreement being reached on global warming. The book goes on to argue that a democratically managed, socialist planned economy can create the conditions where environmental problems are solved.

The publishers, the Socialist Party, its predecessors and international co-thinkers, have always treated environmental questions with the greatest seriousness. Our analysis has consistently highlighted the tendency of competitive capitalist markets to degrade the planet.[2] The present work explains in some detail how and why capitalism has failed to tackle environmental problems and then puts forward a programme for a socialist alternative. It also critically examines how such an alternative system will work. It is hoped that radical Green activists who do not yet consider themselves socialists will be swayed by the arguments.

In attempting to set out a socialist case, it has sometimes been necessary to go into detail. This may require careful study but no apologies are needed for this warning. To present as persuasive an argument as possible requires exploring issues in some depth, not least because of a lack of knowledge of socialist ideas, particularly among young people.

Academic or specialist terms relating to environmental science, capitalist economics, socialism or Marxism are avoided where possible. Readers with a keen interest who are well informed should be able to understand the material. Occasionally though the explanation of a complicated idea has had to assume some specialist knowledge. This is particularly the case in parts of Chapter 5 where some understanding of Marxist economics is needed. Here the reader is directed to publications that explain the fundamentals of the subject. Material of a technical character requiring special knowledge is included in appendices at the end of the chapters.

No attempt is made to hide or to brush over the differences between different trends, tendencies or viewpoints in the environmental or socialist movement. On the contrary, any differences are critically examined. This is because only an open, democratic and healthy clash of ideas can lead to a deeper understanding of the problems we face and create the possibility of finding a way out. The seriousness of the situation calls for nothing less.

As well as radical Greens, the book is aimed at socialists and Labour Movement activists who are concerned about environmental questions. It is hoped that the way the arguments are posed here will help to deepen understanding of environmental relations from a socialist perspective. The broadening of the argument beyond questions directly connected to the environment, to controversies over planning, is intended to contribute to the wider debate on the socialist project. The treatment here will also be useful to students with an interest in the political economy of the environment.

To try to maintain the flow of the narrative, sources and citations have, in the main, only been included where they refer to controversial points or debates. Thanks are due to Judy Beishon, Clive Heemskirk, Pete Mason, Niall Mulholland, Hannah Sell and Lynn Walsh for their helpful comments on the draft of the book. Many of these have been included, but, as usual, all responsibility for the finished article is mine. The assistance of Dennis Rudd from Kavita Graphics was invaluable. Finally, I would like to thank my partner, Kath, for her assistance during the writing.

Pete Dickenson,
London, February 2012.
planning4planet@hotmail.co.uk
www.socialistparty.org.uk/planning4planet
(see website for links to references)

1. See *Planning Green Growth* by Pete Dickenson, London, CWI Publications, 2003.
2. A socialist case on the environment was developed in a publication by the forerunner of the Socialist Party, Militant Labour, more than 15 years ago, (*Global Warning. Socialism and the Environment*, by Martin Cock and Bill Hopwood, London, Militant Publications, 1996).

The author is a university lecturer who researches the impact of the introduction of market systems in the former Soviet Union and China. He also lectures in the field of operations management, which has included teaching environmental management at post-graduate level. He is long standing member of the Socialist Party.

Planning for the Planet: How Socialism Could Save the Enviroment

Introduction

The threat posed by global warming has become the over-riding environmental issue facing the world. As the greenhouse gas emissions that drive global warming have rocketed in the last ten years, the gap between the green rhetoric of governments in the industrialised capitalist countries and their feeble policy response has become a chasm. The 1997 Kyoto treaty was supposed to be the centrepiece of efforts to tackle climate change. After it proved to be totally ineffective the world powers tried to devise a new more effective approach, notably at summits in Copenhagen in 2009 and Durban in 2011. In particular, after ten years of tortuous preparatory negotiations, the Copenhagen meeting's chaotic and ignominious collapse shocked not just most environmental activists, but also wide sections of society worried about the state of the planet their children will inherit. The aim of this book is to explain from a socialist point of view why capitalist society has failed to take meaningful measures to address environmental threats, above all those linked to climate change. The book also argues for an alternative to capitalism, based on public ownership of the decisive sectors of the economy and democratic planning. This will permit action to be taken to stop the degradation of the planet, particularly to reverse global warming, which represents the greatest danger.

First though, the key threats to the environment are summarised in the first chapter. Except for global warming, which has its own chapter due to its importance, the main dangers covered in Chapter 1 are from all forms of toxic contamination, nuclear and non-nuclear, as well as from the destruction and degradation of the earth's natural habitat. Despite the catastrophe at Fukushima in 2011, there is a possibility that nuclear will still be pushed as an alternative to conventional power generation, since it does not generate the greenhouse gases that cause global warming. For this reason, arguments over nuclear power are given prominence in Chapter 1. The pro-nuclear case was given greater credibility when the well known environment writer George Monbiot, in desperation, called its adoption a lesser evil. Monbiot's position is considered and set against the evidence on the dangers of nuclear power, demonstrated by the disasters at Fukushima and Chernobyl and the problems of storing toxic radio-active waste.

The current state of knowledge about global warming and predictions of the effects of climate change are reviewed in Chapter 2. Many environmental activists may think this is unnecessary since the evidence is now overwhelming that increased greenhouse gas emissions are causing global warming. Yet, as the evidence has mounted confirming the link between emissions and rising world temperatures, the claims of climate deniers challenging the basic science of global warming and the dire predictions of its effects, continue to influence many people, including some on the Left. The size of the climate deniers' audience is due mainly to the biased reporting of the conservative media, but the credibility of the deniers is underpinned by growing public scepticism about science, since it is seen as increasingly subject to the demands of the market. Also, carbon taxes, which are, as it will be argued in Chapter 3, incorrectly put forward by most environmentalists as the main way to tackle global warming, are seen by workers and the poor as hitting them the hardest, leading inevitably to further scepticism. For these reasons, the evidence on global warming needs to be objectively reviewed and the arguments taken up.

The review of current knowledge on global warming highlights the dangers of so-called 'tipping point' effects, that could mean present predictions of global temperature increase and its consequences are underestimated. This raises the possibility that the effects of climate change are already irreversible. The implications of this are considered, in particular whether policy should be focussed on ways to adapt to climate change rather than on its mitigation.

Chapter 3 reviews the policy response by governments since global warming emerged as a serious issue 20 years ago. It analyses the paradox faced by the world's ruling classes, most of whom realise that it is necessary to take measures to tackle climate change, but are impotent to act. What Kyoto was and how it was supposed to work is taken up. Its failure and the failure of its intended successor, the Copenhagen Treaty, to get off the ground is then analysed from a Marxist point of view. The position of some on the Left that the capitalist class can be pressurised to take radical 'green Keynesian' measures to tackle climate change is considered, as are the likely implications of this approach. In conclusion, it is argued that while capitalist relations persist there is a tendency to appropriate and degrade the environment. Due to competitive pressures, market approaches or regulation applied in a capitalist context are unable to overcome environmental degeneration. This is a truth revealed graphically by the fiasco of the UN sponsored Copenhagen summit in 2009.

The inability of the market system to tackle climate change, explained in Chapter 3, poses the need for international socialism. This could allow decisive action to be taken to tackle global warming, by removing rivalries between the main imperialist powers and unleashing the potential of democratic planning. Chapter 4 first makes this case for a socialist alternative to tackle climate change and then outlines the measures that will be needed to put a new system into practice. The programme outlined will, it is argued, enable greenhouse gas emissions to be hugely reduced in a planned programme over several decades.

Two of the common criticisms levelled at implementing such a radical new approach are answered. They are first that the costs involved will be huge and will hit living standards and second, that a switch to a green economy will lead to big jobs losses. Costs are analysed at a national and international level, as well as sector by sector for the branches of the economy affected. Set against this is an estimation of the savings that will accrue when the waste and misallocation of resources that characterises the old market economic system is ended. The implication for jobs of a socialist programme for the environment is also analysed for key industrial sectors.

To recap, in Chapter 3 it is argued that the capitalist market system is destroying the environment. This failure is linked to the antagonism between nation states that prevents agreement on global warming in an imperialist epoch, and more fundamentally to the inexorable tendency of competitive markets to degrade the environment. To address these problems requires, first of all, a progamme, which is outlined in Chapter 4. Its basis is ultimately to take into public ownership the big corporations that dominate the world economy in order to break the destructive power of the market. This then poses the requirement for an alternative way to organise the economy, which, unlike capitalism, will allocate resources to meet human needs, the most profound of which is to ensure the survival of life on the planet in the long term. As the only alternative to the market, it is proposed in Chapter 5 that a system of planning can efficiently allocate resources to meet need, as well as conferring other big environmental advantages, but only if it is organised democratically.

To help illustrate how planning techniques can be applied, the theories of Wassily Leontief are explained. He began to develop his Input-Output theory based on initial research in the Soviet Union in the 1920s and eventually published an environmental treatment of the theory in the 1970s. Detailed studies are given to show how planning will work in a contemporary industrial economy. A key theme is that although modern communication and computer technology, such as the internet, will greatly facilitate the efficient operation of the plan, more important than the technical detail is the political context of planning, if it is to be effective. It is proposed that the creation of institutions to allow the democratic control by workers and consumers of all aspects of the planning process, at all levels, is vital if the failures of previous attempts at planning are to be avoided.

Chapter 6 considers some controversial issues about the limits to growth and the viability of socialist planning. Many environmental activists, including those on the Left, think that to tackle global warming, cuts in consumption, possibly very big ones, are necessary. Even more Greens think that it will be impossible for countries such as China and India to enjoy the standard of life in industrialised nations without destroying the planet. These ideas are challenged from a socialist viewpoint, as are claims that the environmental crisis can be solved by controlling population growth.

Objections to a planned economy have existed as long as have the socialist ideas that first questioned the beneficial role of capitalism. In particular, a fierce controversy developed in the 1920s and 1930s between supporters of planning and its opponents that became known as the 'socialist calculation' debate. The arguments involved, which were at a mainly theoretical level, are explained and the lessons brought out, since they are still very relevant today. As well as the theoretical objections to planning that were encompassed by this argument, critics also focus on the failure of the Soviet bureaucratic command economy as proof, they claim, that planning will not work. These criticisms are answered by examining the history of planning in the Soviet Union and linking the ultimate failure of the economy to the degeneration of the country into a Stalinist dictatorship, which it is argued, is not an inevitable outcome of a socialist society. Chapter 7 concludes by issuing an urgent warning to the Labour Movement that it must take responsibility for addressing climate change, because any further delay will produce a catastrophe for the planet.

Chapter 1:
The Planet in Danger

Few on the Left and certainly no environmental activists argue against the view that we face an environmental crisis. So, whilst it is not required to prove here that there is a catastrophe looming, it is nevertheless useful to summarise what the key threats are. It is also necessary to assess, critically where appropriate, what science is telling us about the dangers we all face. It is useful to summarise the key threats because it will help put into context the economic and political arguments related to the environment that are the main themes of this book. It is also necessary to assess the science used to understand the dangers facing the planet because it is increasingly being challenged, most prominently by the climate change deniers. Their claims have to be taken up since they sometimes gain undeserved credibility, due to the public scepticism of science engendered by modern capitalist society.

Apart from global warming, the other significant dangers we face are pollution linked to nuclear power generation as well as from many other causes, including the release of genetically modified organisms (GMOs). Deforestation and desertification threaten the environment and the lives of the poorest on the planet, both phenomena being linked to global warming, as is accelerating species extinction. The oceans and the living organisms in them are under attack from many directions including fishery destruction and toxic pollution from various sources, not least oil spills, highlighted by the Deepwater Horizon disaster in the Gulf of Mexico in 2010. Also still a threat, although now rarely commented on, is the break-up of the ozone layer in the upper atmosphere. This was caused historically by the release of chemicals called CFCs that were used to power aerosols. CFCs have now been banned, but it will take up to 100 years to repair the atmosphere, during which time skin cancer rates will increase in many parts of the world. Leaving aside climate change for the moment, the other threats will now be considered, starting with contamination linked to nuclear power generation.

1.1 The dangers of nuclear power

After decades in decline following the Chernobyl catastrophe of 1986, nuclear power was again promoted by many governments as the threat of global warming increased. This was because its use does not result in the release of significant quantities of the greenhouse gases that cause climate change. Nuclear was given increased credibility on the left when the well known environmental writer and campaigner George Monbiot backed it as a lesser evil. Regardless of Monbiot's desperate U-turn, it would be completely wrong to assume that this option does not pose a massive threat to the environment. The danger is comparable, arguably albeit on a lower level, to that of global warming, since it is linked to the dangers of accidents like at Chernobyl and Fukushima in Japan and the problem of disposing of toxic waste. (See boxes on Chernobyl and Toxic waste).

The nuclear disaster at Chernobyl in the Ukraine in 1986 was the worst in history

What happened at Chernobyl

The Chernobyl catastrophe was the world's worst nuclear accident. The explosion at the power plant, situated about 100 miles north of Kiev in Ukraine, then part of the Soviet Union, sent a cloud of radioactive gas around the world that contained twenty times the amount of radiation released at Hiroshima. Estimates made at the time in *New Scientist* that 100,000 would eventually die as a direct and indirect result of the radiation release may have been too high, but if the wind had been blowing in the opposite direction on the day, towards the densely populated city of Kiev instead of over relatively sparsely inhabited areas, the outcome would have been worse than even the *New Scientist* estimate.

The reactor at Chernobyl was a boiling water, graphite moderated type called a RBMK, many of which are still in operation in the states of the former Soviet Union (the final reactor at the Chernobyl power station was only shut down 15 years after the incident). It is inherently unsafe in a nuclear reactor to have high temperature graphite close to steam under pressure, but this is what happens in the RBMK. In this type of reactor, the uranium fuel rods are surrounded by graphite, that absorbs some of the heat of the nuclear reaction, a process essential to control its speed. Boiling water is pumped past the fuel rods and graphite to carry away more of the heat, and the steam produced is used to drive turbines to produce electricity. In addition, the graphite has to be surrounded by helium and nitrogen gas to stop it burning in the surrounding air. If the hot graphite and the uranium rods come into contact with the steam an explosion is possible, producing a cloud of radio-active steam, which is exactly what happened in April 1986. The scale of the accident was made worse because there was no containment structure around the reactor, which could have prevented the steam from escaping into the atmosphere.

The immediate reason for the explosion lay in the effects of a sudden power surge causing a rupture in the pipes holding the cooling water, thus bringing it into contact with the graphite. The power surge occurred in the first place because of a reckless experiment that was being conducted by technicians on an under-power reactor, that was aimed at speeding up the time it took to repair faults. The technicians were scapegoated at the time, but the reason they were conducting the experiment in the first place was linked to the then power crisis in the Soviet Union. Nuclear stations are usually operated to provide 'base load' electricity, that is they are operated 24 hours a day because it is difficult and time consuming to stop and start a reactor. If there are frequent faults which means that the reactor has to be switched off, its efficiency is drastically reduced. As a result, the technicians were under pressure to come up with a quick and easy answer to the problems caused by the frequent faults in the power plant.

Western observers at the time highlighted features specifically linked to the Soviet system that contributed to the disaster, such as the reckless behaviour of the staff, driven by an impatient, bullying bureaucracy, themselves pressurised by the deep problems in the economy, combined with the poor design and unreliability of the power plant. However, the underlying cause, which was a combination of human error and mechanical failure, was the same as occurred at the major nuclear accident in the USA at Three Mile Island in 1979. The nuclear plant there was based on a PWR (Pressurised Water Reactor), the same type that is used at the Sizewell power station in Britain. During the crisis at Three Mile Island, the radio-active material at the core of the reactor came within 700F degrees of its melting point of 5000F. If such a meltdown had occurred there would have been a major disaster, possibly worse than at Chernobyl, since the melting uranium could have penetrated deep into the earth, in the process contaminating ground water over a wide area.

The Danger of Toxic Waste

Advocates of nuclear power will point to the low theoretical risk of an accident happening, but this must be set against the potentially catastrophic scale of any incident when it does occur and also the risks of nuclear power generation not directly connected to the safety of the operation of the plant. These are primarily linked to the problems of safely reprocessing and storing the toxic waste that is produced as a by-product of nuclear power.

Potentially even more serious than the health problems linked to low level radiation leakage associated with reprocessing, is the issue of storing toxic nuclear waste. A direct consequence of producing electricity with nuclear reactors is the accumulation of radioactive waste, uranium and plutonium. Apart from electricity generation, there is a significant amount of plutonium produced for military purposes which also has to be stored. To give an idea of the scale of the problem, the amount of toxic nuclear waste stored in the USA in 1991 was 4900 cubic metres with a radioactivity of 24,000 MCi (A Curie is a quantity of radioactivity, MCi is one million Curies). To put this in perspective, a typical radioactive source used in a classroom for a science experiment has an activity of one millionth of a Curie. An average sized 1000 megawatt (MW - one million watts) nuclear power station reactor has a total radioactivity of 70 MCi in its spent fuel one year after discharge. After 100,000 years this figure will fall naturally to 2000 MCi, still two billion times more radioactive than a typical source used in a classroom. (There is far more waste to store now of course, compared to 1991, and the amount is increasing all the time.)

The implication of this data is that a safe storage method must be found that can be guaranteed to be secure for more than 100,000 years, a task that poses huge uncertainties and problems because it is difficult to predict what natural conditions will be after that time. If the waste is buried, the onset of earthquakes in previously unaffected areas is possible, as is a meteor strike. If the radioactive spent fuel is put at the bottom of the ocean the integrity of the materials used as a storage medium must be uncertain after such a long time, possibly leading to seepage. Also undersea volcanic activity could start, producing the same result. No safe storage method has yet been found, which is an unsolved problem that it would be irresponsible to add to by generating yet more waste.

Fukushima disaster

It was a tragic coincidence that the nuclear disaster at Fukushima occurred within weeks of the 25th anniversary of the catastrophe at Chernobyl. When the scale 9.0 earthquake struck just off the coast of the Japanese city of Sendai on Friday 11th March 2011, the seismic shock was immediately registered by the sensors at the Fukushima 1 plant, which is situated on the coast, south of the epicentre of the quake. This had the effect of shutting down the reactors as a precautionary measure. Dozens of pro-nuclear experts then kept assuring TV viewers that 'everything was under control'. However, after the control rods had been lowered into the reactor core to stop it functioning, it was vital that the cooling system kept operating, because the fuel rods continue producing significant amounts of heat due to the on-going nuclear reaction, (see diagram). If this was not done then the heat would boil off the water covering the reactor core, which could then melt down, penetrate the containment structure and release radiation to the atmosphere. The quake had cut off the electric power supply to the cooling system, but the diesel powered back-up then cut in as planned, so things still seemed to be under control.

After the nuclear disaster at Fukushima in Japan in 2011 it took nine months to stop toxic radio-active waste leaking out of the plant

Unfortunately the earthquake was followed by a tsunami, which easily overcame the coastal defences around the plant and inundated the reactor buildings, putting the diesel generators out of action. All that was left now was a third line of defence, a room full of batteries, but these lasted for only a few hours. As John Gittins, former safety director of the UK Atomic Energy Authority, explained, quoted in *New Scientist*, the only option was to try to pump sea water into the reactors to cool them.

This was difficult because as the pressure in the core rose it became ever more difficult to force the sea water into the vessel. Also, the heat was by then so great the sea water evaporated more quickly than it was pumped in, and "that heat makes xenon and krypton gas inside the fuel rods exert a positive pressure, cracking some of the zirconium alloy fuel rod capsules".

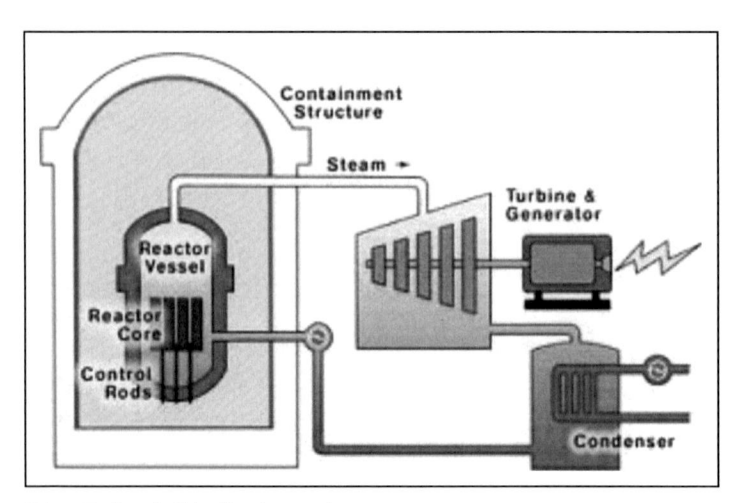

Schematic view of a Fukushima-type reactor

Radioactive caesium and iodine fission products could then escape from the rods and into the steam, which was vented from the containment vessel to stop it exploding. This did not however prevent the outer buildings surrounding the containment structures blowing up when the steam was vented, since highly explosive hydrogen was also generated by the conditions. No-one could assert any longer that the situation was under control.

Part-used nuclear fuel, such as that found at Fukushima, contains several radioactive isotopes with different toxic effects. Iodine 131, which was released at Fukushima and at Chernobyl, although in far greater quantities in the Ukraine, is absorbed by the thyroid gland and can cause cancer, particularly in children. Caesium 137 was also released in Japan and Chernobyl, but it was not definitively linked to cancer at Chernobyl, although this may have been due to poor health data. Measurements by the Japanese Ministry of Science, analysed by *New Scientist* at the time, showed that concentrations of radioactive caesium 137 reached similar levels to those after the Chernobyl catastrophe. Up to 50km from the plant, well outside the original official exclusion zone, the figure was 6400 kBq/sq.m., whereas at Chernobyl, the most highly polluted areas were defined as those with a concentration of 1490 kBq/sq.m. of caesium. (i.e. 1490 times a thousand[k] Becquerels of radiation per square metre. A Becquerel, Bq, is a unit used to measure the amount of radiation). Caesium 137 has a half-life of 30 years, meaning it is significantly radioactive for this period, and so is potentially dangerous for longer than the other chief radioactive isotope released at Fukushima, iodine 131, that has a half-life of 8 days.

Fukushima 1 had 6 reactors, three of which were operational at the time of the earthquake, but, as it later emerged, trouble also arose with the stored spent fuel, that is housed in the same buildings as the reactors. There was a meltdown of the nuclear fuel in reactors 1 and 2 and 3. The buildings housing the reactors 1 and 3 were destroyed by hydrogen explosions, as steam was vented into these areas from the containment vessels.

The situation in the reactor 4 building was potentially very serious, with a possible hydrogen explosion in the area storing spent fuel rods, leading to a fire. The spent fuel area did not have a containment structure around it, so radiation from the ponds holding this fuel could have been released directly to the atmosphere. There was a danger also that as these rods heated up, they could go 'critical', starting a nuclear chain reaction (although a nuclear explosion was not possible). This scenario arose when it was revealed that the entire core of reactor 4 had been put into the storage ponds, creating a potentially critical mass.

There was a scandalous lack of data made available by the private operator, the Tokyo Electric Power Company. This organisation had, in the late 1980s and 1990s, been found to have systematically falsified records of safety problems at its nuclear reactors. It also admitted that it was unaware that its Kashiwazaki Kariwa facility was built immediately above an active fault line, where four tectonic plates converged. When an earthquake hit that nuclear plant in 2007, it was put out of action for two years.

Nine months after the Fukushima disaster, the Japanese government finally announced that significant radioactive leakages had been stopped, although it would take 40 years to clean up and decommission the plant.

At Fukushima, there were clear similarities with the Chernobyl disaster, since design flaws played key roles in both disasters. In Japan, the chief flaw was that the multiple backup safety systems should not have had causes of failure in common. The earthquake toppled the power lines that cut off electricity to the cooling system and the resulting tsunami put the diesel backup power out of action, in other words the failure of both systems had a common cause. Backup independence could have been achieved with higher walls protecting from a tsunami, or simply putting the back-up power generators on high ground.

There were multiple design flaws in the Chernobyl reactor, the most serious being that the reactor core did not have a containment vessel around it at all. A similar situation was found at Fukushima, where the spent fuel storage area, where a fire started and radiation was emitted, also did not have any containment around it.

However, because at Chernobyl the reactor itself was unprotected, more radioactivity was released there than in the Japanese plant. Nevertheless, the two accidents were both rated as 'level 7', the highest possible.

The key point is that it is very difficult to predict every possible situation that in extremely rare circumstances could lead to failure. But when these circumstances arise, as they inevitably have been seen to do, a catastrophe is possible. This is one of the fundamental problems with nuclear power. Since Japan is one of the most technologically advanced countries on earth, so theoretically should have been able to design out failure, the situation in some other countries using nuclear power will be even more dangerous. For instance, China is planning a crash programme of building new nuclear reactors, far outstripping all other nations, but despite strict environmental regulations on paper, laws are commonly flouted at local level, in the 'wild-west' capitalist atmosphere that exists there.

Controversy over extent of nuclear danger.

The nuclear lobby at first claimed that the release of a significant quantity of radiation was highly unlikely in Japan due to the fail-safe design of the reactors, but then retreated to a second line of defence when this was shown not to be the case. Their new position was that even if large amounts of toxic material had been given off, the dangers to health were acceptable, particularly when compared to the risks associated with energy generation from fossil fuels. Leading this defence was George Monbiot, who previously had credibility among green activists as a campaigner against global warming. He called the claims about the number of deaths associated with low-level radiation, such as that linked to caesium and iodine isotopes, as grossly exaggerated and 'a fairy-tale'[1]

It is true that the estimates of deaths resulting from Chernobyl have varied widely, from the UN report in 2008 that estimated a final death toll of 4000, to the claim made in an article in the *Annals of the New York Academy of Science* that nearly a million have already died.[2] So far, 6000 thyroid cancers have been recorded due to Chernobyl, and a recently published peer-reviewed article, based on research funded by the US National Institute of Health, found that the number of new thyroid cancer cases linked to the Ukrainian disaster is not falling.[3]

Elizabeth Cardis, from the Centre for Research in Environmental Epidemiology in Barcelona estimated that there will be 25,000 cancer cases by 2065, although the UN report says there is no persuasive evidence for this. Regarding the variability of the predictions, Cardis made the point that the evidence is fragmented and contradictory, partly because research did not begin until many years after the accident. She was calling for a new definitive study to be made, but it is unlikely that the true picture will ever be established, due to the chaos that engulfed the collapsing Soviet Union in the years after Chernobyl.[4] Many of the people affected dispersed over the vast area of the USSR and subsequently the world, and will never be traced. This particularly applies to the tens of thousands of so-called 'liquidators', the army conscripts who were drafted in to fight the accident and who were exposed to very high levels of radiation, without being told of the dangers.

Monbiot's assertions of a relatively low death toll were based on the absence of Western peer reviewed articles in the medical and scientific press confirming the higher figures and continuing scientific controversy about the dangers of low-level radiation. Leaving to one side that research conducted in Eastern Europe but not published in peer reviewed journals in the West is not necessarily wrong, the subsequent chaos in the region and the extremely belated start of systematic research meant that it was always going to be very difficult to satisfy the very stringent methodological criteria required by most Western publications. Set against the lack of Western published material, there have been a large number of local studies carried out in the areas affected pointing to a high eventual death toll, plus significant anecdotal evidence of the devastating effects on the health of the population in Ukraine and Belarus.

In the context of the uncertainty surrounding the eventual number of victims and the ongoing scientific controversy on the effects of low-level radiation, at the very least a precautionary approach is required when assessing the dangers of a nuclear accident. Monbiot accepted such an approach when the evidence on global warming was still inconclusive and fragmentary, on the grounds that the potential danger was so large. Surely the same logic applies to the effects of nuclear radiation and the higher casualty estimates therefore should be taken seriously? Also, when assessing the dangers of nuclear, a power station accident is only one factor, more serious in the long run, as has already been discussed, is the problem of safely storing toxic nuclear waste, which will remain radioactive for more than 100,000 years. Existing toxic waste will have to be dealt with, but it is irresponsible to advocate creating even more in these circumstances.

Even if George Monbiot's unlikely claim is true about a final Chernobyl death toll of 'only' 4000, this does not justify his support of nuclear energy. He invoked a balance of risk argument to compare this figure to the likely devastation caused by global warming, since nuclear power does not produce greenhouse gases and therefore is a possible alternative to burning fossil fuels. It is true that global warming could create more victims than even the highest estimate of the death toll at Chernobyl, but the implication of Monbiot's position is that there are only two options; nuclear power or burning fossil fuels. Renewable energy can do the job (see Chapter 4), as he was arguing himself at one time, only to reject it as 'unrealistic', since governments were not willing to pay, since they preferred cheaper nuclear power.

1.2 Toxic environmental contamination

Thousands of toxic substances produced by the world's chemical industries are released every year, which threaten the earth's air, land and sea. Some discharges hit the headlines like oil spills (see box on Deepwater Horizon disaster) or the leaks of radioactivity at Fukushima. However, the volume of contaminants released in less dramatic circumstances far exceeds these high profile cases and overall more damage is probably caused. These cases include industrial discharges, sea dumping, spillages and the effects of pesticides and synthetic fertilisers.

> **Deepwater Horizon disaster**
>
> There was an explosion on a BP oil rig in the Gulf of Mexico in 2010 when 11 workers were killed. BP initially said that only a thousand barrels per day of crude oil were being released, but subsequently experts calculated that the figure was as high as 62,000 barrels a day, a huge difference that it was impossible to check at the time since the company refused to allow access to independent scientists and engineers to perform their own tests. Deepwater Horizon was the most serious oil spill in US history, totalling 205 million gallons, by far exceeding the previous worst, the pollution from the Exxon Valdez tanker accident off the coast of Alaska in 1989 which released 11 million gallons.
>
> Capping the well to try to cut off the leak took 3 months and oil was still leaking out months later. It took so long because the leak was 5000ft down on the sea bed. A further complication was that the hurricane season was just beginning in the region which compounded the technical difficulties.
>
> The Gulf of Mexico is an important habitat for endangered sperm whales, sea turtles and blue fin tuna which were all under threat from the oil leak as were sea birds. Six months after the leak, the official toll was 6000 dead birds, 700 sea turtles and 101 dolphins, porpoises and whales. This though was probably a major underestimate of the true death rate, since many animals after ingesting oil just sank to the bottom of the ocean.[5] In March 2011, a paper in the journal *Conservation Letters* concluded that the mortality of dolphins and whales as a result of the spill may have been 50 times higher than the original estimate and up to five thousand dolphins alone may actually have been killed.[6] Oil poisons the coastal sea floor, interrupting the food chain that marine life depends on and ultimately threatening the extinction of species and organisms like coral. A team of researchers lead by Charles Fisher of Penn State University found many recently dead colonies of coral and others that were clearly dying, that Fisher put down to the effects of the spill. The coastal fishing industry also was devastated as fish were contaminated and tourism hit hard as recreational fishing had to be abandoned.

Poor regulation was blamed for the accident as there were scandalous failings in this area. The Minerals Management Service (MMS), the government body responsible for regulation, had been described as corrupt by Friends of the Earth and even the US President complained, after the event, of the cosy relationship the body had with Big Oil, the multinationals that dominate the industry. A US government report on the MMS found that there was a 'revolving door' of oil company executives joining the agency, watering down the regulations and then going back to their original companies on higher salaries. BP applied for a drilling permit for this project to MMS in February 2009, stating that it was 'highly unlikely that an accidental oil spill will occur' and even if it did, BP would be able to fix it. This was accepted at face value by the MMS and no further details were asked for, although BP later admitted that it was not prepared for the accident. The regulatory failures just masked though the underlying cause of this accident: that profit hungry corporations will put the environment at the bottom of their priorities and exert their influence over governments in order to water down and bypass any rules.

Genetically Modified Organisms

The release of genetically modified organisms (GMOs), must also be added to the list of potentially dangerous contaminants. Genetic engineering has the possibility to transform medicine and other aspects of our lives for the better, but its main application to date has been driven by agribusiness to generate quick returns, for example in the manufacture of disease resistant strains of crops. This may seem a progressive development, but there are possible dangers attached to the use of GMOs, linked to their ability to interbreed with natural organisms and spread through nature in unpredictable and uncontrollable ways. Since the long term effects when this happens are still not clear, they should not be deployed in agriculture until there is sufficient scientific knowledge to permit their safe use.

One of the arguments put forward by the manufacturers in support of GMOs is that they are urgently needed to eliminate world hunger, since they increase the output of crops. (So, in the eyes of the producers at least, presumably justifying the risk.) The GMO supporters' position is undermined though by data from the UN Food and Agriculture Organisation, which pointed out that one and a half times the food required to feed the population of the planet is already being produced, so removing the urgent need for genetic engineering to increase food production. Hunger persists because of a disfunctional capitalist socio- economic system, in all its manifestations, not because of an insufficient capacity to turn out food.

Ozone Depletion

As already briefly mentioned, a serious continuing danger that should also still be highlighted is linked to the discharge of CFCs, chemicals that previously were used to power aerosols. Their effects continue to pose very serious dangers, although they are rarely mentioned now, since the problems connected to them were thought to have been solved. The layer of ozone gas in the atmosphere protects humans and the ecosystem from the harmful effects of the sun's radiation and it was damaged by the release into the atmosphere of CFCs. An international agreement called the Montreal Protocol was designed to cut and eventually eliminate the production of CFCs and had an effect, since their output fell by 77% between 1988 and 1994. (Incidentally, this may appear a successful example of international capitalist co-operation, but to what extent it is a model for international agreements to tackle environmental problems is considered in Chapter 3.)

Despite the action that was belatedly taken, the result of the delay was that the full recovery of the ozone layer is not expected to take place until the 22nd century, because there is a long lag before the levels of chlorine in the stratosphere, that the CFCs produced and which caused the ozone break-up, return to normal. This meant that the benefit of the first reductions in CFCs that took place in the 1980s were not apparent until the early 21st century, and until chlorine levels are back to normal in the next century the ozone layer will continue to be attacked. The 3% loss of ozone noted in 1991 over the USA was expected to produce 12 million extra skin cancers in that country alone.

1.3 Destruction of the natural world.

Deforestation, fisheries destruction and species depletion are manifestations of the accelerating degradation of the natural world. The Amazonian rainforest has been reduced in area by 15% and that in Indonesia by 72%,[7] caused by encroachment of agricultural land for cattle grazing and particularly for soya and palm oil production. Logging, legal and otherwise, is another major threat, which in turn is linked to land speculation, money laundering connected to the drugs trade and corruption and tax evasion. Brazil is claiming that her action to stop rain forest destruction is having an effect, but this will probably only be temporary. This is because the commodity-led boom in the local economy, linked to Chinese growth, has pushed up the value of the currency and made agricultural exports less profitable, so reducing pressure to turn forests into agricultural land. To get round the problem of currency appreciation hitting profits, the government is moving to further deregulate and weaken environmental laws, which are already significantly under-enforced.[8] When the currency eventually falls in value, the pace of destruction will again accelerate, made even worse by the additional deregulation.

The area of the Amazonian rainforest has been reduced by 15%

The land grabs which contribute to deforestation are being driven mainly by commercial interests, many linked to multinational corporations, but there are also some desperate landless agricultural workers who are taking over and cultivating former rainforest. Although it is outside the scope of this book to develop the point, their interests can be met without destroying the forests, but only through a radical programme of land reform. Deforestation is also made worse by global warming, but at the same time it is contributing to the problem, issues that will be taken up in the next two chapters.

Fisheries Destruction

It has been claimed that the biggest single threat to the marine ecosystem is from over-fishing.[9] Modern factory ships, using sonar technology to detect shoals and massive trawling equipment that can reach the sea floor, are destroying whole populations of fish. 90% of large fish such as tuna, cod and halibut have been wiped out, which is causing a shift in the ocean ecosystem to one in which small plankton eating animals predominate, such as jelly-fish. Tens if not hundreds of thousands of jobs have been lost as the Newfoundland, North Sea and Baltic Sea fisheries have largely collapsed. The attention of the big companies has now turned to the Pacific, the only remaining area not yet fished out, but the same fate awaits this region as befell the North Sea, if the present profit driven approach is not fundamentally changed. Unless this happens, all that will remain on the menu before long may be jelly-fish and chips.

Deforestation and fisheries depletion are part of a wider picture of habitat destruction that is driving the reduction in bio-diversity. 20,000 species a year are being lost according to Douglas Crawford-Browne, Director of the Cambridge Centre for Climate Change Mitigation.[10] He and most environmentalists blame this situation on 'human action', but in fact it is a very particular form of 'human action' that is in the dock, i.e. the pursuit of profit in a capitalist market economy. The vast majority of the problems discussed here can be traced back to the detrimental activities of big business, particularly multinational corporations and their agents. We have seen this above, whether the problems are linked to over-fishing, deforestation or toxic contamination, of nuclear and non-nuclear origin. The irresponsible action of private business was particularly highlighted by the role of the firm running the Fukushima power plant, which was discussed earlier. But despite the devastating evidence of the danger of atomic power generation, most governments still want to retain it as an alternative to burning the fossil fuels that cause global warming. The activities of corporations and the governments that represent their interests illustrate a key theme of the book, which is that competitive markets degrade the environment.

One vital environmental question not yet considered is the looming threat posed by global warming. Due to its significance this will be dealt with in Chapter 2.

1   Quoted in the *Guardian* 6/4/11.
2   Alexey V. Yablokov, Vassily B. Nesterenko, and Alexey V. Nesterenko, (2009), 'Chernobyl: Consequences of the Catastrophe for People and the Environment' *Annals of the New York Academy of Sciences*, Volume 1181, December. Consulting Editor Janette D. Sherman-Nevinger (Environmental Institute, Western Michigan University, Kalamazoo, Michigan.)
3   Brenner A.V. et al, (2011), 'I-131 Dose-Response for Incident Thyroid Cancers in Ukraine Related to the Chernobyl Accident', *Environmental Health Perspectives*, Vol. 119. March 17.
4   http://www.newscientist.com/article/dn20275-act-now-to-track-health-effects-of-nuclear-crisis.html
5   http://www.greenpeace.org.uk/media/reports/deepwater-horizon-one-year
6   Rob Williams et al, (2011) 'Underestimating the damage: interpreting cetacean carcass recoveries in the context of the *Deepwater Horizon*/BP incident' *Conservation Letters* Volume 4, Issue 3, pages 228–233, June/July 2011. Article first published online: 30 MAR 2011
7   http://www.greenpeace.org/international/en/campaigns/forests/threats
8   *Financial Times* Special Report, Sustainable Business, 29/11/11, p3
9   http://www.greenpeace.org/international/en/campaigns/oceans/overfishing
10 Quoted in the *Financial Times*, Special Report, Managing Climate Change, 28/11/11, p3

Chapter 2:
The Critical Threat of Global Warming

The devastating floods in Pakistan in 2010 and Hurricane Katrina in the USA in 2005 highlighted the possibility that climate change, manifested in extreme weather events, is with us now. This shattered any remaining complacency that it is a problem for future generations. Meteorologist and former Hurricane Hunter Dr. Jeff Masters argues that "it is quite possible that 2010 was the most extreme weather year globally since 1816 (http://thinkprogress.org/romm/2011/06/24/253299/masters-driven-by-global-warming-it-is-quite-possible-that-2010-was-the-most-extreme-weather-year-globally-since-1816/). Although some think these were isolated events unconnected to environmental changes, research after Katrina in particular made a strong case that the warming of the ocean was leading to more severe hurricanes (see box on Hurricane Katrina.) There is now sufficient evidence for climate scientists to call for extreme weather events to be considered as related to global warming until proved otherwise, rather than the other way round.[1]

In the 1990s, the evidence that dangerous global warming was taking place was even then very strong, but not overwhelming. Consequently, the need for action was posed in a precautionary way, in the sense that since the threat was so potentially catastrophic, it was necessary, even in the absence of overwhelming evidence, to assume the worst would happen. Since then, as will be shown, the scientific data has grown to the extent that there is no longer reasonable doubt that the earth's temperature is rising rapidly. The need to rely on a precautionary approach to urge rapid action has therefore disappeared.

The scientific underpinning for belief that the temperature rise is caused by human action has also grown, so that recourse to precautionary arguments is no longer necessary here either. In the same period, however, although predictions of the effects of global warming have become much more accurate and soundly based, there inevitably has remained a degree of uncertainty about predicting events decades or even centuries in the future, given our current level of knowledge. Climate deniers, often linked to vested interests in the oil industry, have used this remaining uncertainty to continue to challenge the scientific basis of global warming. They rely on increasing public scepticism of science to get an audience for their ideas, including from some on the Left, often influenced by post-modernism. For this reason, it is necessary here to take up the main arguments put forward by the sceptics, after briefly reviewing the latest evidence on climate change and the urgency of the situation.

Global warming and Hurricane Katrina

There is evidence that global warming will make, and possibly is making, hurricanes more destructive than they would otherwise have been, according to climatologists writing on the Real Climate website.[2] Their argument is that rises in sea surface temperatures (SST) are linked to the power of hurricanes, because warm water, and the instability in the lower atmosphere created by it, is the energy source of hurricanes. This is why hurricanes only arise in the tropics and during the time of year when sea temperatures are highest which is June to November on the US Atlantic seaboard. One cause of rising SSTs is the increased level of carbon dioxide in the atmosphere due to the burning of fossil fuels, i.e. global warming. (Apart from high SSTs, changes in wind strength and direction at different levels in the atmosphere, called wind shear, influence the formation of hurricanes by preventing the development of the organised wind patterns that are necessary for them to form. Changes in these wind shear effects have not been linked so far to global warming.)

Computer models, similar to the one used to predict Katrina's path, that allow for the effects of climate change, have indicated that more intense, although not more frequent, hurricanes will occur. The models predict that the frequency of the strongest category 5 hurricanes triples when the effects of human induced global warming are factored in. Although recent scientific papers have reported that there has been no increase in Atlantic hurricane activity in the past century, over a time when carbon dioxide emissions linked to global warming have been increasing rapidly, closer analysis reveals that this evidence does not contradict a possible global warming link. This is because only the frequency of all tropical storms was measured, not changes in their intensity. The computer models that predict a link to global warming only predict an increase in the frequency of the most severe category of storms, not in the frequency of hurricanes in general.

An article in July 2005 in the science magazine *Nature*[3] confirmed that there is a link between hurricane intensity and rising SSTs. The author concluded that as tropical SSTs have increased in the past decades so has the intrinsic destructive power of hurricanes (measured by the power dissipated by the storm, the so-called power dissipation index). It is disputed whether the rise in SSTs is due to human induced global warming or to natural fluctuations in surface temperatures. The National Hurricane Center in the US has asserted that the recent upturn in hurricane activity has been due to natural fluctuations. However, Kerry Emanuel, the author of the article mentioned above in Nature argues against this being the only cause of increased sea temperatures. Emanuel measured the power dissipated by storms, and the change in SSTs, over the past 80 years and found that the dramatic increase in both over the past 10 years was well outside the fluctuations found in the previous 70 years. From this it was concluded that "the large upswing in the last decade is unprecedented, and probably reflects the effects of global warming". A common theme of many recent publications on the future of tropical cyclones globally is that the total number of these storms will decrease, but the strongest storms will get stronger. (http://thinkprogress.org/romm/2011/06/24/ 253299/masters-driven-by-global-warming-it-is-quite-possible-that-2010-was-the-most-extreme-weather-year-gl obally-since-1816/) Most notably, in 2010 there was Super Typhoon Megi. Megi's sustained winds cranked up to a ferocious 190 mph and its central pressure bottomed out at 885 mb on October 16, making it the 8th most intense tropical cyclone in world history.

2.1 Time rapidly running out to take action

What is Global Warming?

The greenhouse effect is a process that keeps our temperature about 30C warmer than it would be otherwise, a difference needed to support life. In the 19th Century scientists realised that the atmosphere allowed more incoming radiated heat from the sun than it does outgoing radiation, so trapping heat inside the earth's atmosphere. Figure 1 is a simple diagram that explains this. Also in the 19th Century, the greenhouse gases that caused the heating effect were discovered, the main one being carbon dioxide. Carbon dioxide is largely the result of burning fossil fuels, such as coal, gas and oil, but there are other significant greenhouse gas culprits such as methane, which mainly occurs naturally. As the concentration of greenhouse gases rises, the amount of heat trapped in the atmosphere also goes up, in a fixed relationship, and leads to a rise in temperature, although not in an easily predictable manner. Since the early 20th Century, global temperatures have risen rapidly, so far by 0.7C (See Figure 2). A rise of 0.7C may not seem big, but this needs to be compared to the figure of 2C, beyond which it is widely accepted that global warming effects could become irreversible.

The Greenhouse Effect

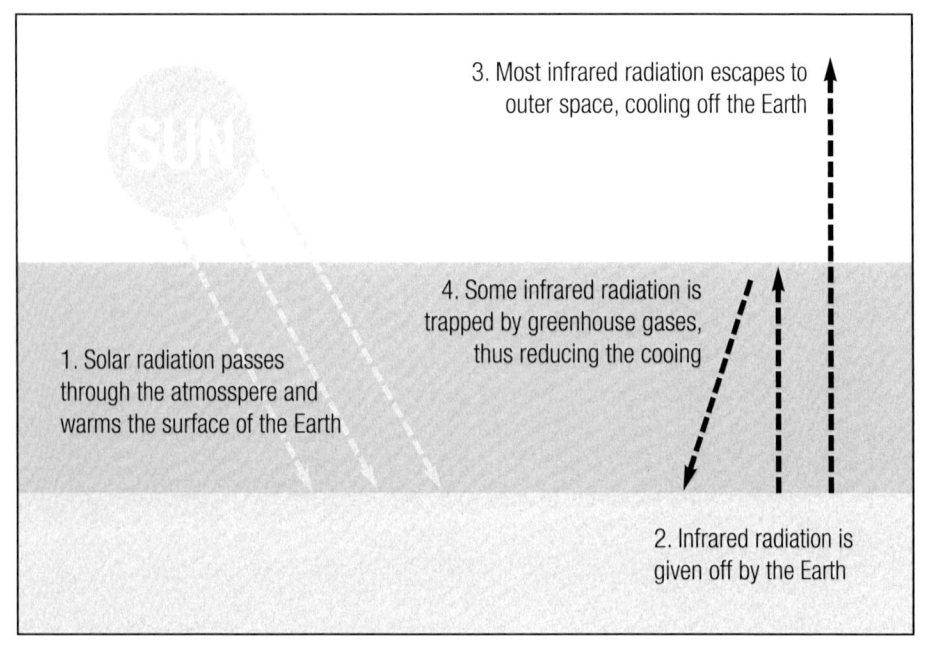

1. Solar radiation passes through the atmosspere and warms the surface of the Earth
2. Infrared radiation is given off by the Earth
3. Most infrared radiation escapes to outer space, cooling off the Earth
4. Some infrared radiation is trapped by greenhouse gases, thus reducing the cooing

Figure 1: The Greenhouse Effect. (From the Stern Report[4])

Predictions of future warming cover a big range, depending on the assumed sensitivity of the earth to the concentration of greenhouse gases in the atmosphere. The present concentration is about 430 parts per million in the air, of what is termed carbon dioxide equivalent.(i.e. 430ppm CO_2e). The CO_2e, or equivalent unit, is often used so that the whole range of greenhouse gases, most significantly methane, is taken into account. It has been estimated that a figure of 400ppm could result in temperature rises of between 0.6C and 4.9C depending on assumed sensitivity and a concentration of 1000ppm could produce rises in the range of 2.2C to 17.1C[5]. The International Energy Agency estimated in 2006 that emissions will more than double by 2050 on current trends, which could result in a temperature rise of between 1.7C and 13.3C[4] according to these calculations. Also, the predictions here could be conservative because of so-called tipping point effects.

Tipping Points

Tipping points, that are sometimes called positive feedback effects, reinforce global warming in various ways. For instance, the role the oceans currently play in absorbing carbon dioxide could be switched to one of emitting the gas. This could happen because as sea temperatures rise due to global warming itself, the oceans' ability to absorb further

The Critical Threat of Global Warming

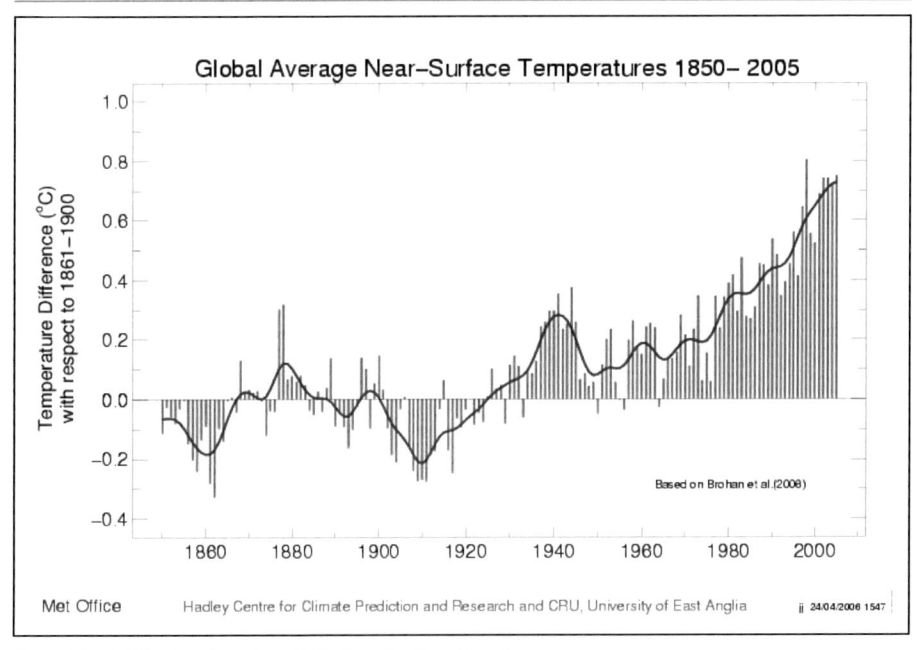

Figure 2: Global Warming since about 1900. (From the Stern Report)

carbon dioxide is reduced. Another serious tipping point threat is the possible collapse of the global ocean circulation system which may shut down not only the Gulf Stream but also effect the Asian monsoon, leading to warming of the Southern ocean and destabilisation of the West Antarctic ice sheet. At the same time the El Niño current in the Pacific could become a permanent feature, hastening the disappearance of the Amazon rainforest, an important absorber, or sink, of CO_2. Already, the Amazon has turned into a net emitter of carbon dioxide during two monster droughts in the first decade of the 21st Century. Connected to the disruption of the ocean currents is another tipping point that is linked to the melting of the polar ice, whose absence, because it is no longer there to reflect the sun's rays back beyond the atmosphere, will further reinforce global warming.

Perhaps the most serious positive feedback phenomenon however, although the most unpredictable, is the release of methane into the atmosphere. Methane has a far more toxic effect than carbon dioxide in relation to global warming and potentially vast quantities could be released as the earth warms. Methane presently trapped in the permafrost is equivalent to double all the greenhouse gas emissions yet made and it is not clear to what extent it will be released as temperatures rise in permafrost regions. Yet even more methane is under the oceans, kept in place by sufficiently low temperatures and high pressures, but if ocean warming penetrated deeply enough it is theoretically possible that some of this gas could be released with catastrophic effects.

Effects of Global Warming

There is a wide range of predictions cited above of possible temperature rises, because estimations depend on assumed sensitivity of the earth to rises in greenhouse gas concentrations. Sensitivity to greenhouse gases is an area that is not yet fully understood, but if the upper end of the estimates, 13.3C, proves to be true, it will be difficult for life to be sustained on the planet. Although this extreme outcome is statistically unlikely to happen, it is nevertheless a warning of the profound dangers we face. A recent lower prediction, that is much more likely, and which would nevertheless still be devastating, is for a rise of 4C by 2055 made by the UK Met Office, a leading authority in climate science.

According to Wolfgang Cramer at The Postsdam Institute for Climate Research in Germany, a 4C rise would mean 83% of the Amazon rain forest destroyed by 2100.[6] His colleague at Potsdam, Anders Levermann, has developed a model that is predicting alternating extreme monsoons and droughts in China and India that will threaten irrigation systems and access to drinking water. Overall, lack of water, crop failure and rising sea levels could force up to 200 million people from their homes by 2050. The Stern Report[4] into climate change, commissioned by the New Labour government and then ignored, assuming a 2-3C rise, also predicted more frequent droughts and floods. In addition, Stern warned of declining crop yields and fish stocks and from tens to hundreds of millions flooded out of their homes. Climate change will also increase deaths from malnutrition, heat stress and diseases such as malaria and dengue fever. In a nutshell, the effects of global warming will be devastating and borne mainly by the poor.

Is it too late to do anything?

The evidence that there is a rapidly worsening situation, combined with the threat posed by tipping point effects, raises the question whether it is too late to take action on climate change. The Intergovernmental Panel on Climate Change (IPCC), the leading international climate body under the auspices of the UN, concluded in its report in 2007, that some effects of global warming were indeed now irreversible. Further light was thrown on this conclusion by researchers in the USA, France and Switzerland (see box on Irreversibility).

To what extent is global warming irreversible?

Carbon dioxide concentrations will remain high for at least a thousand years even if greenhouse gases are eliminated in the next few decades, according to researchers in the USA, Switzerland and France. Also, the climate scientists who produced this claim are asserting that the effects of global warming, such as high sea levels and reduced rainfall in certain areas, will also persist over this time scale. (The findings are in a paper in *Proceedings of the National Academy of Sciences*[7]). The authors of the paper make various estimates of CO_2 concentrations based on the year emissions are cut, assumed to be from the years 2015 to 2050. They make conservative assumptions, for instance, that emissions are cut at a stroke rather than gradually and that their annual rate of growth before cut-off is 2%, not the 3%+ witnessed from 2000-2005. They then estimate what the effects would be on surface warming, sea level rise and rainfall over a thousand year period using the latest climate models. The results of the melting of the polar ice caps are not included in the calculations of sea level rise, only the expansion of the water in the oceans caused by the surface temperature increase. As the authors point out, the actual new sea-level will be much higher.

The 'best-case' results for surface warming, those where action is taken in 2015 to eliminate emissions, show that over a thousand years the temperature falls from 1.3 to 1.0 degree above pre-industrial levels. The 'worst-case', where action is delayed to 2050, predicts surface temperatures will increase from just under to just over four degrees by 2320 and then remain approximately constant for the rest of the millennium. High levels of CO_2 persist in the atmosphere because over long time scales reduction of the gas is dependent on the ability of the oceans to absorb it. There are limits to how far this can go due to the physics and chemistry of deep-ocean mixing. On the other hand, the amount of heat in the atmosphere that can be absorbed by the sea, the key way surface temperatures are decreased, is limited by the same scientific laws. As a result, carbon concentrations cannot fall enough to force temperatures down and there is simultaneously reduced cooling due to limited heat loss to the oceans.

The data for sea level rises are even more disturbing, with the 'best-case' showing a small rise over the millennium of .35 metres compared to pre-industrial levels and then stabilising, but the 'worst-case' has sea levels elevated by nearly 2 metres in the year 3000 and still rising. There is a theoretical possibility that the melting of polar ice could add several metres to these figures, but the very long-term effects of increased CO_2 concentrations on melting rates are not well enough understood to make firm predictions in the authors' opinions.

The research also makes estimates of precipitation (rainfall) changes over the next millennium. As the authors acknowledge, on a small scale and for many regions of the world, it is still not possible to make predictions in this area. However, since the fundamental physics is well understood - that increased temperatures cause increased atmospheric water vapour concentrations - and due as well to advances in modelling, some long-term trends can be identified. These show a pattern of drying over much of the already-dry subtropics in the latitudes 15^0 to 40^0 in both hemispheres. Seven regions are identified as at risk: south-east Asia, eastern South

> America, southern Africa, the south-western USA, western Australia, northern Africa and southern Europe. The reductions in predicted dry-season precipitation range from 3-6% in the 'best-case' to 15-35% in the 'worst-case', and within these ranges, the most badly hit regions are expected to be northern Africa and southern Europe.

Most estimates of the longevity of global warming effects, after greenhouse gases have been removed, have ranged from a few decades to a century, so this analysis could represent a development with very serious implications, including political ones. Clearly, predicting so far into the future must be subject to uncertainty given the accuracy, although rapidly improving, of existing climate models. However, the assumptions made are conservative and the science the models are based on is well established, so the results must be taken seriously. Seeing this data, climate sceptics may now say it is pointless doing anything to mitigate global warming effects since they are irreversible or at least will persist for a thousand years. However, the analysis shows that the severity of threat will vary enormously depending on when decisive action is taken. So if emissions are eliminated in 2015, the effects, even if they last for a 1000 years, could be manageable, since temperature rises will peak at less than the widely accepted tipping point of two degrees. But if nothing is done before 2050, a catastrophe will loom since surface temperature is predicted to rise by over four degrees.

This research undermines the market-environmentalist theory that it will be possible to tackle warming only at some unspecified point in the future, when incomes have risen. This position is based on the so-called 'environmental Kuznetz effect', named after a well known economist. The theory claims that rises in incomes have been linked empirically to lower pollution. Even if true, in the light of the profound economic crisis that began in 2007, it is a particularly dubious assumption that individuals will inevitably be richer in the future on a capitalist basis. Clearly if action is delayed for a prolonged period of time while capitalism is given time to recover and incomes theoretically to rise, it will be too late to stop an environmental disaster.

Geo-engineering

If nothing meaningful is done over the next decades and a climate disaster results, then the ruling classes may be tempted to resort to panic measures that promise a quick fix to the problem. Indeed, right-wing think-tanks, mainly in the USA, are already pushing for so-called geo-engineering solutions, such as seeding the atmosphere to simulate the effects that follow a major volcanic eruption. They see this as a solution because of the observed temperature fall after such explosions. In 1883 a volcanic explosion at Krakatoa, off the coast of present day Indonesia, was the most

Ash from volcanic eruptions can lower temperatures. Reckless right-wing pressure groups want to mimic this effect to tackle climate change

severe is recorded history, with the noise of the explosion heard in Australia. Millions of tons of volcanic ash shot into the atmosphere that wind currents subsequently carried round the world. Significantly for the discussion here, it was noticed that there was an effect on climate, because heat from the sun was reflected back into space by sulphate particles in the ash.

More recently, after the eruption of Mount Pinatubo in the Philippines in 1991 that sent huge amounts of sulphate particles into the stratosphere, the Earth cooled by a few tenths of a degree for several years. This may seem small but is significant in global warming terms. The proposal now by some scientists is to mimic the effects of a volcanic explosion by pumping sulphate particles into the atmosphere to reproduce its cooling effects. Research though in the scientific journal *Geophysical Research Letters*[8] has shown that this could have severe consequences. The study by researchers at the National Centre for Atmospheric Research in Colorado into the after-effects of the Pinatubo explosion found that there was a marked decrease in rainfall. They concluded that any attempt to inject sulphate particles into the stratosphere could have a disastrous effect on the Earth's water cycles, leading to catastrophic drought and famine.

Another problem linked to this type of experiment is that if carbon levels continue to rise, it would require ever increasing 'fixes' of sulphate particles injected into the atmosphere. If they were ever stopped, there would be a sudden and very large rise in temperature. Despite these dangers, sections of big business see geo-engineering as a cheap and quick fix to climate change. For instance Bill Gates, founder of the Microsoft company, and well-known entrepreneur Richard Branson are funding research into this area. In Russia, a climate sceptic and senior advisor to the government has already started testing the effects of spraying sulphur particles from a helicopter.[9] (It is never explained why climate sceptics think such drastic measures are needed to fix a problem they say does not exist, or at least is hugely exaggerated.) The growing interest by the capitalists in a supposed 'quick and cheap fix' to global warming threatens a nightmare future that could almost be as bad as climate change itself. However, if the current diseased system remains in place, where profits are paramount, then the chance of such desperate measures being seriously contemplated will remain. This scenario is not inevitable, but to avoid it will require removing the fundamental cause of the problem - the capitalist market system. The longer the Labour Movement takes to address this task the worse the prospects will be for the environment.

2.2 The Climate Deniers

The predictions and analysis made in this chapter assume that the reader has been prepared to believe the data presented and the good faith of the scientists behind it. On both counts, however, there is an increasing challenge by climate deniers, often funded by the oil companies, who question not only the data but the motives and integrity of the climate experts. Before looking to see if there are any grounds to their claims, one question needs to be asked: should the ideas of climate deniers be addressed at all, given their vested interests in oil companies and links to extreme right-wing think tanks? Would taking them seriously give undeserved credibility? This is the position of many environmental activists who quite correctly say that the deniers' theories have virtually no credible support in the scientific community. On the other hand, it is necessary to consider the growing public scepticism about science, including climate science, a scepticism shared by a few on the Left and some working class people. Such scepticism, as well as reflecting a wider crisis of legitimacy affecting all bourgeois institutions, is found on the Left due to the increasing abuse and debasement of science by big business. For this reason alone it is necessary that the position of the deniers is considered.

The controversy that surrounded the leaked emails from climate researchers at the University of East Anglia (UEA) in 2009 gave the sceptics a huge boost in credibility. The deniers argued that the leaked emails seemed to show that manipulation, or at least suppression of data, had occurred in order to support theories of human induced global warming. Subsequent enquiries found that there was no substance to the charges made against UEA, but damage had been done to climate science since there was a clear lack of transparency in the dealings of the experts. The confidence given to the sceptics by this episode led to a new scrutiny of the findings of the most authoritative climate science body, the Intergovernmental Panel on Climate Change (IPCC). This resulted in its report in 2007 being castigated in sections of the press for publishing unsubstantiated data and misleading the public about the dangers of global warming. The newspapers attacking the IPCC were well known climate deniers, but in the aftermath of the UEA Climategate row their claims were given wide prominence.

New Scientist magazine analysed the IPCC report and the reliability of the data on which it was based. The magazine found, significantly, that the section on the physical science of climate change, rather than on its effects, went largely unchallenged, even by the climate denying press. The controversial part of the report were the predictions on the likely effects of global warming, in particular regarding water supply, food and bio-diversity. On the latter, the claim was made by the IPCC that 20%-30% of plant and animal species face extinction if temperature rises exceed 1.5-2.5 degrees above present levels. This figure was based though on only one scientific paper that predicted global changes. The rest of the data was derived by the IPCC from other studies that only looked at regional figures or those for particular species. Also, the methodology of the paper on global changes was criticised in several subsequent papers. However, when the authors of these critical articles were contacted, none objected to the IPCC findings and one said that its conclusions were too cautious.

Of the other two areas scrutinised, food and water supply, there was evidence that the conclusions reached were unjustified and somewhat exaggerated. On the effects of climate change on drought in Africa, it was stated that an average of 152 million people would suffer from increased 'water stress'. This conclusion however ignored other available data from the same cited paper that showed increased access to water in some African regions. The IPCC report also did not reflect the warning in the paper not to take its projections too literally. There were similar problems with the part of the IPCC report dealing with food, in particular in the projections for crop yields in Africa, where it was stated that yields in some countries could be reduced by 50% by 2020. However, the research that was quoted in the report was not peer reviewed for accuracy and validity by other scientists, as would usually be the case, which casts doubt on the reliability of its conclusions. Not being peer reviewed does not necessarily mean findings are wrong, but *New Scientist* also found other problems. The research only referred to crop yields in rain-fed regions of Africa, whereas in large areas of the north of the continent crops are irrigated rather than rain-fed. The IPCC ignored this distinction, which undermined the validity of their headline conclusion of a 50% fall in yields. Other criticisms that were given press prominence were found to reflect more minor errors, such as the statement that 55% of the Netherlands is below sea-level, rather than 55% will be at risk of flooding.

Subsequently, in 2010, it emerged that the claim made by the IPCC that the Himalayan glaciers will disappear by 2035 was not supported by the available evidence, although they are under threat. The public scepticism towards science that allowed sections of the climate-change denying media to exaggerate, sometimes hysterically, the errors in the IPCC report, is ultimately a reflection of a crisis of legitimacy of bourgeois capitalist society. (See box Can scientists be believed?)

Can scientists be believed?

The public scepticism of science is ultimately a reflection of a broader crisis of legitimacy of bourgeois society. This is characterised by an increasing questioning of claims made by the ruling class in many spheres of life, for example, in politics, law and economics, as well as in science and medicine. The array of experts lined up before the Iraq war of 2003 to 'prove' that WMD existed fuelled this new mood, as did the assurances of some scientists that genetically modified organisms are safe to consume. Many on the Left share the mood of scepticism about science, since they see the pernicious effects commercialisation has had. A report by Scientists for Global Responsibility[10] highlighted five sectors where commercialisation has impacted science: pharmaceuticals, tobacco effects, oil and gas, defence and bio-tech.

Chemical engineering and geology are strongly linked to oil companies and many university engineering departments have funding from the arms industry. Also, life science departments in universities have extensive links to bio-technology and pharmaceutical industries. The report says this has created enormous conflicts of interest that are undermining the quality and reliability of research, resulting in 'sponsorship bias' where research generates results that suit the funder and in failure to report unfavourable results to the sponsor. Research aimed at short-term commercial gain is crowding out 'blue skies' studies and work on environmental and social issues. For example, Scientists for Global Responsibility found genetics now dominates agricultural research since it is patentable and therefore potentially lucrative, whereas studies of low intensity agriculture are sidelined.

In medical and environmental research, tobacco and oil companies have spent millions to deny the links, respectively, between smoking and lung cancer and human induced climate change. Considering the commercial motives undermining science, it is not surprising that even some socialists take a sceptical attitude. It would be a mistake however to judge the validity of an argument primarily on the motives of those making it, even though motivation as a factor should not be ignored. Climate deniers are not wrong per se because they are funded by oil companies, but because their arguments do not hold water. Some on the Left, influenced by post modernism, have questioned the validity of science, with its replacement of objective truth by 'competing discourses', where motivation is regarded as paramount, but to do this is a profound mistake.

Marx described science as the handmaid of capitalism and in this role it has been shaped, and ultimately distorted and corrupted to an extent in its quest to interpret and understand our material existence, particularly in the epoch of capitalism's decline. It will only be with the removal of the distortions caused by commercial motives that science will become fully objective. Nonetheless, scientific investigation remains rooted, in the final analysis, in a materialist approach to achieving understanding and as such retains its validity. This is because capitalists, despite corrupting science for short-term economic gain, need to increase productivity to survive in a competitive system. Exploiting the forces of nature through science is a key way to achieve this. This requires that scientific ideology keeps its objective and material basis.

To illustrate the point, compare science in capitalist society today with that in ancient Greece. There, alongside profound scientific insights, that endure today, existed fantastical and mystical ideas, apparently without contradiction. This was possible because science existed largely in the realm of ideas, there was no call to challenge contradictory positions because there was little need to harness science to the needs of society. The economic imperative in ancient Greece was to ensure the continuing supply of slaves, which did not require the intervention of science by and large. In modern capitalism the economic imperative is to maximise profits and a key way to do this is to increase the productivity of labour, a task in which there is limited room for distortion, idealism or mysticism in science.

Public scepticism, to an extent understandable, means that advocates of action on climate change must be very careful not to lay themselves open to allegations of bias or misrepresentation. In particular, predictions of the future effects of global warming must be treated very carefully, since current models cannot predict with great accuracy events decades in the future. However, it is still absolutely clear that climate change effects are getting extremely serious, made even more worrying by their relative unpredictability.

2.2.1 The arguments of the climate deniers

The deniers have taken three basic positions; first denying that global warming is happening at all, then saying that it is a natural phenomenon, not human induced and finally down-playing the seriousness of its effects. As the evidence has mounted supporting the idea that the threat is real and due to human intervention, they have retreated from one position to another. There are however those who still deny that the Earth's temperature is rising, like Fred Singer, founder of the think-tank Science and Environmental Policy Project. Since 1979, he says, the global climate has if anything cooled. So let us examine the scientific evidence of global warming in more detail.

To what extent is global warming human induced?

Due to lack of data, the debate in the 1990s was inconclusive over the extent to which global warming is caused by the emissions of greenhouse gases that began in the industrial revolution. It was claimed by sceptics that the evidence about when global warming began was contradictory, citing a paper in the science journal *Nature*, that studied temperature changes over the past millennium. The paper indicated that global warming began in 1600. This would mean that the rise in the Earth's surface temperatures was not due to the greenhouse effect, since carbon dioxide levels did not begin to increase significantly until the industrial revolution 150 years later. This evidence would also support the view that the 20th century was no warmer than the 11th, and that the 1990s was not the warmest period in history, the contention of the sceptics in the so-called 'hockey stick' controversy. In fact real doubt has been cast on some claims made by climate scientists on this subject. For instance, it now looks as if there was not enough evidence to say the 1990s were definitely the hottest recorded. However, although natural effects, such as solar activity, do effect global temperatures, sometimes significantly, an analysis of solar activity over the past 30 years would predict a fall in temperature rather than the observed rise. In truth, there are no natural effects that could have caused the increase of 0.5C in temperature that has been observed in just 30 years. The claim of the deniers was decisively refuted in 2005 by research in the USA and Britain reported at a meeting of the American Association for the Advancement of Science in Washington and subsequently published in the scientific press.[11]

Strong evidence was presented, which indicated that global warming is due to human activity. The new findings came from studies of variations in ocean temperatures that used 7 million readings stretching over 40 years. It is important to analyse changes in these temperatures because 90% of heat from the planetary warming of the past forty years has gone directly into the oceans, the conference heard. At the meeting, scientists from the Scripps Institute of Oceanography in San Diego argued that each of the oceans warms differently at different depths and therefore provides a fingerprint to help identify the causes of global warming. For instance, particular patterns of temperature variation with depth and position are associated with particular causes such as natural variation, solar changes or volcanic effects. The model that most closely matched the fingerprint however was that for global warming. What struck the researchers was the remarkably close statistical fit of the data with the global warming model, leading them to dismiss any other reason for the observed water temperature rise.

How dangerous is global warming?

The final redoubt of the deniers is to challenge the extent of the threat produced by global warming. Here there is considerable scope for argument because both sides inevitably have to speculate about events sometimes far into the future where it is difficult, if not impossible, to reach unequivocal conclusions. However, despite the uncertainties that sceptics latch onto, a review of the findings of nearly 1000 articles on climate change in peer-reviewed scientific journals (i.e. ones that have been scrutinised by other leading scientists for their accuracy), by Naomi Oreskes of the University of California, San Diego, showed that there was a near universal consensus opposing the sceptics' position. The climate change deniers counter with personal attacks and sweeping assaults on the integrity of the scientists and their publications. They claim that virtually all climate scientists are biased due to politically motivated, pre-conceived ideas and some even allege an enormous conspiracy after the furore over Climategate, but subsequent investigations showed there was no evidence for this claim.

Another line of attack the deniers use is to argue that the current scientific consensus on global warming cannot be invoked to prove the case. It is right, of course, that science is not conducted by consensus, since new truths usually emerge from the clash of competing ideas that can continue for years or decades. However, this does not mean that this particular consensus is wrong! All claims must be viewed ultimately, although not uncritically, on their own merits, and the evidence for human induced warming is overwhelming. Indeed, 25 years ago this theory itself was supported by just a tiny minority and only became accepted as the evidence mounted to back it, something that has not happened to competing cooling theories.

Even though evidence is mounting all the time that restricts the sceptics' room for manoeuvre, there is always going to be a degree of uncertainty about the long-term effects of human induced temperature rises. This does not mean though that action does not need to be taken urgently. For example, consider the scientific controversy over the link between smoking and lung disease that stretched over decades, which has some similarities with the current dispute. The scientific 'deniers' of the link between smoking and cancer were often paid by the tobacco industry and the evidence at first was not completely clear cut, which gave the industry a chance to refute the claims of the anti-smoking lobby. Even now the exact mechanism of how smoking causes cancer is not fully understood - for instance, why some people smoke heavily all their lives and do not develop the disease. However, a lack of a complete picture did not prevent a scientific/medical consensus emerging that demanded decisive action be taken. It is true that the uncertainties of predicting the effects of climate change, decades or even centuries in the future, are greater than those surrounding the smoking/cancer link. But global warming is proven and the consequences of not taking action are potentially more disastrous, even threatening the continuation of life on the planet in the long term.

New Technology

One of the lines of argument of the sceptics in downplaying the seriousness of global warming is to argue that humankind will be able to cope with its effects using new technology. This raises the question of how likely is it that technology will emerge to solve the problem of global warming. Of course, renewable power generation technology exists now, such as wind, wave and solar power, but it is relatively expensive to introduce.

What the capitalist system is looking for is an invention that can generate sustainable energy that is as cheap or almost as cheap as using oil. In search of this promised land, research has continued for decades into the possibility of developing as an energy source nuclear fusion, which has the potential to produce virtually unlimited amounts of power with no pollution. The basis of the technology is to try to harness the vast amount of energy released when atoms are fused together, which unlike splitting the atom, does not produce toxic radio-active waste. The leading capitalist countries realised early on that international co-operation would be needed, because massive resources were required to give a chance of success in tackling this very complex problem. However, partly as a result of squabbling between the partners over who would pay what, the deployment of the money, and over the long-term future of the programme, no decisive breakthrough has been made.

2.3 Decisive action needed now

The Stern report concluded that cuts in greenhouse gas emissions of 80% are needed to stabilise carbon dioxide equivalent levels (which include the effects of other greenhouse gases such as methane). If decisive action was taken to achieve this, in five to ten years after 2007 when the report was published, then temperature rises could be limited to less than 2C and the worst effects of global warming avoided. In these circumstances, it would wrong to bow to the idea, now promoted by climate deniers, that adapting to climate change is more important than mitigating its effects and that resources should be directed to adaptation. It is true that some global warming effects are already irreversible and will have to be dealt with, but these should not be unmanageable if effective action is taken soon. To abandon attempts to stabilise emissions is therefore not justified. Even if the situation becomes much more serious due to a lack of prompt action, it will still be necessary to cut greenhouse gases in order to achieve long term stabilisation, at the same time as adapting to climate effects.

As the dire consequences of global warming increasingly become clear, sections of big business and some in the governments that represent it, will look to geo-engineering measures as a quick and cheap fix. This nightmare possibility could result in outcomes that are nearly as bad as climate change itself and reinforces the need for urgent and effective action to reduce emissions. The prospects for such action are considered in the next chapter.

1   See *New Scientist*, 28th August, 2010, p14.
2   Go to: www.realclimate.org
3   See *Nature* 436, 686-688 (4 August 2005)
4   *The Economics of Climate Change. The Stern Review*, by Nicolas Stern, Cambridge University Press, 2007.
5   Figures taken from a book published in 2006 that reviewed 11 recent studies. (Meinshausen M, 'What does a 2C target mean for greenhouse gas concentrations? A brief analysis based on multi-gas emission pathways and several climate sensitivity uncertainty estimates', in H J Schellnhuber et al, (eds.) Avoiding dangerous climate change, Cambridge, Cambridge University Press, p265-280)
6   Professor Cramer was speaking at the 4 Degrees and Beyond, International Climate Conference, 28-30 September 2009, Oxford UK. For details go to: http://www.eci.ox.ac.uk/4degrees/downloads/programme.pdf
7   Go to www.pnas.org/cgi/doi/10.1073/pnas.0812721106 for full article.
8   See: *Geophysical Research Letters*, Vol. 34, L15702, 5 pp., 2007, doi:10.1029/2007GL030524. 'Effects of Mount Pinatubo volcanic eruption on the hydrological cycle as an analog of geoengineering' by Kevin E. Trenberth and Aiguo Dai.
9   See *New Scientist*, 17 July 2010, p22.
10 See *New Scientist*, November 7th 2009 for a report.
11 For a summary go to: http://www.aaas.org/news/releases/2005/0217warmingwarning.shtml and for the full article: http://journals.ametsoc.org/doi/full/10.1175/JCLI3723.1

Planning for the Planet: How Socialism Could Save the Enviroment

Chapter 3:
How Green will the capitalists go?

Like many previous summits, the 2011 UN sponsored climate change conference in Durban, South Africa, abjectly failed to reach an agreement to tackle global warming. Despite this outcome, the chair of the conference said at the end, referring to a 'Plan A', which was supposed to be legally binding rather than a 'Plan B' which would have been voluntary: "...we have concluded this meeting with Plan A to save our planet for our children and grandchildren. We have made history" (*The Times* 12/12/2011). Chris Huhne, the then UK Energy and Climate Change Minister added, "This is the first time we have seen major economies commit to take action demanded by the science"(*New Scientist* 17/12/2011).

Anyone knowing the seriousness of the environmental situation would have had to assume that both these statements reflected either the deepest political cynicism or self-delusion almost on a level requiring medical intervention, since nothing substantive was agreed on either count, legal or scientific. All the conference ended with was a hope that a new and as yet unspecified agreement to replace the Kyoto climate reduction treaty, which ended in 2012, would come into operation by the earliest in 2020. That is, no new deal will be in place before then, when climate science says that the greenhouse gases causing global warming must be cut by 40% by 2020 to avert a potential catastrophe. The wording agreed to form a legally binding basis for a future treaty was so vague as to be worthless.

Despite the failure at Durban and the shambolic collapse of the Copenhagen summit in 2009, events that seemed to have exposed the limits that the ruling classes were prepared to go to address global warming, most capitalist politicians and commentators nevertheless continue to pay lip service to tackling global warming. Some even seem to understand that meaningful action is required to try to prevent a looming catastrophe, judging from their dismayed reaction to the Copenhagen summit in particular. So, leaving the lessons of Copenhagen aside for the moment, what prescriptions are being proposed and what chance of success do they have?

3.1 Can market-based approaches tackle global warming?

Despite the failure to produce results, the dominant approach to tackling climate change and other environmental issues remains rooted in using market approaches. The 'command and control' methods of direct regulation used by the bourgeoisie from the 19th Century onwards have been largely cast aside since the sharp ideological swing to the right in economics over the last 30 years.

Property rights

The classic method put forward by the neo-liberal school to take account of environmental damage is the so called 'property rights', sometimes called 'public choice', approach, which relies on direct negotiations between the parties affected to resolve the issue. Capitalist commentators generally, and especially neo-liberals, always emphasise the sacrosanct nature of private property, which explains why this is their preferred approach. (Private property is defined here as the means of production, i.e. factories and so on, and not as the personal property of individual workers.) The public choice method requires that the property rights to the use of environmental resources are defined and owned by someone. If ownership can be established, then, according to the capitalist economic theories, the bargaining between the property owners will produce an 'efficient' outcome.[1]

'Efficiency' here though is defined as the result of the narrow pursuit of individual economic self-interest in a bargaining process, ending in the outcome where all possibilities for mutually beneficial exchange have been exhausted, therefore giving an 'optimal' result. This is a consequence of the balancing of the economic self-interests of the property owners. It does not claim, even on its own terms, to produce an equitable environmental outcome that reflects the needs of society as a whole. The examples that are used to prove the property rights theory are extremely simplistic. They hardly ever approximate to anything like a real life situation, and so it is easy to see the practical difficulties in implementing the approach. For instance, it is hard to imagine what system of private ownership could be imposed on the overheated stratosphere. Even if it was, the number of people affected by this 'market failure' runs into billions, in fact the entire population of the planet, all of whom could seek redress from the owner. This would make the method patently unworkable. Another problem is that to get an 'efficient' outcome, any negotiating is meant to be between free and equal parties. This is a fantasy, of course, certainly in terms of climate change. The chief victims of global warming will be poor, flood-plain dwellers in places like Bangladesh, whereas their counter-party in bargaining could be a multinational corporation in the USA.

Incentives to stop polluting

The practical difficulty in using the property rights approach has even struck some die hard free-marketeers and an alternative system based on controlling pollution through the price mechanism has been proposed. This is the so called 'make the polluter pay' principle, a theory coming from neo-classical economics.[2] (See box on neo-classical approaches.)

> ### Neo-classical approaches
>
> The principle of carbon taxes is that by increasing the price of polluting resources, there will be an incentive created to use them less and seek substitutes. At the centre of the theory is the concept of 'externalities'. An example is where a firm, as a result of its production, damages a third party at no cost to itself. In an environmental context, this clearly applies to greenhouse gas emissions where a firm burns fossil fuels, causing society as a whole to suffer. However, there is no market-based way to stop this. This 'market failure' arises because environmental goods are not, and generally cannot be, priced.
>
> The task of neo-classical theory then is to find a way of putting a monetary value on the costs of fixing global warming and the benefits that accrue to the polluter. If this can be done then a tax or charge can be levied on the polluter, directly or indirectly, at a level that produces a cost-benefit balance and so results in an 'efficient' outcome. At discussed above, this efficient outcome does not claim to be environmentally equitable for society. All it does is produce an outcome where the environmental damage is limited to the extent that costs and benefits are balanced (costs and benefits are expressed in what are called marginalist terms in neo-classical theory[3]).
>
> A big problem that arises is how to meaningfully measure costs in money terms. In practice, costs have to be estimated by a roundabout route by establishing a 'shadow' market value. This value is usually related to how much a consumer is willing to pay for environmental 'goods' or to avoid environmental 'bads', or to accept compensation to give up the former or suffer the latter. These figures are determined in a survey, producing though wildly different estimates of willingness to pay for the same thing, varying by up to 400 times.[4] This approach is problematical as well in a more general sense, since it incorporates the usual assumptions of neo-classical economics. First, it assumes individuals act alone to calculate their economic advantage in making choices in the market. This 'rational agent' theory produces a decision making process where human agency is reduced to individuals responding to price signals, where there is no place for the interests of society. Just as problematical is establishing a shadow value over time, since issues linked to climate change for example will persist for many generations, if not centuries.

A meaningful shadow market value, to the extent it exists at all, can only be properly assessed by successive generations, whose 'willingness to pay' could vary dramatically according to how the environmental crisis develops. Since future generations have no 'rights' as consumers, applying neo-classical theory to allocate resources 'efficiently' between present and future generations makes no sense. Establishing the costs of climate change over time, in the sense they are discussed here, in practice is virtually impossible, as many commentators, including those not on the Left, have pointed out.[5]

Permit Trading

Despite the manifest drawbacks, there is a near consensus among the ruling classes that there is no alternative to using neo-classical market instruments to tackle climate change. The preferred route this takes is by the trading of pollution permits. These are issued by government to achieve a price supposedly reflecting the environmental costs and cover a specific geographical area and produce an 'efficient' outcome. Leaving aside for the moment the fiasco of the Kyoto permit trading experience, it is not difficult, in the light of the comments above, to see that this scheme would be ineffective. For instance, the cost of building flood defences in Bangladesh in 20 years time, needed because of global warming due to emissions by US corporations today, would not be included in the permit price, meaning that the polluter is not really paying at all. In practice, the price of permits is fixed by political considerations rather than mythical efficiency criteria, which amounts to keeping the price as low as

Speculators have made millions trading in 'permits to pollute'

possible to encourage recalcitrant countries like the USA to take part in the process. Needless to say, the market price has never been at a sufficiently high level to make firms reduce their greenhouse gas emissions and to seek greener substitutes.

Eco-taxes

An alternative to the permit system is the introduction of a carbon-tax, although this is regarded as a dangerously 'socialist' idea by the neo-liberals, compared to the free trading of permits. This is despite the fact that this instrument sits firmly within the framework of neo-classical market failure theory, in terms of seeking 'efficient' outcomes. It smacks, though, to neo-liberals too much of government intervention compared to permit trading, and as a result has never been attempted to any significant extent.

Some eco-economists, recognising the limitations of market failure theory, advocate that eco-taxes should be set according to social and environmental criteria rather than 'efficiency' ones (or in addition to, as most advocate) in order to have a chance of tackling global warming. It is true that if eco-taxes were set at sufficiently high levels they could under certain circumstances force corporations to change their behaviour in a greener direction, but a closer look at the issue reveals big problems if this is attempted.

Evidence to show eco-taxes work is put forward by comparing the experience of the USA and some other advanced capitalist countries. Energy prices in the USA are a third of those in countries like Norway, whereas US emissions of carbon are about three times greater per unit of GDP,[6] thus, it is argued, the tax mechanism seems to work.

The issue is not so simple however when examined in more detail. France, for instance, has a relatively good greenhouse gas performance because it introduced nuclear power on a massive scale, which does not produce greenhouse gases. This was done for political reasons, not because the price of fossil fuel was high, therefore questioning the link between high fossil fuel cost and low pollution emission. Also, the evidence shows that key economic factors that help create sustainability, e.g. the development of new non-polluting technology, would not be promoted to a significant extent by adjusting prices through eco-taxes.[7]

It is not clear how 'price sensitive' consumers will be to eco-taxes, i.e. how much they will be incentivised to become greener by changes in prices. This is important because the changes needed to tackle global warming are large, i.e. a cut in greenhouse gas emissions of at least 70%, and this cut will have to be achieved relatively quickly, by 2050. Could eco-taxes deliver this radical transformation? There is evidence that the patterns of demand in the areas needed to achieve environmental objectives are not price sensitive. A reason for this has been put down to the 'embeddedness' of particular commodities in technologies, infrastructures and social systems.[8] Unless this factor changes, demand for products will not alter much, since consumers are 'locked into' certain patterns of consumption. Examples could be car use, demand for agro-chemicals or oil for energy or industrial production.

Most consumers do not have the option of 'choosing' a green energy supplier and the net result of an eco-tax, certainly in the short or medium term, i.e. in the years to 2020, would be little reduction in greenhouse gases. The same logic applies to public transport, where a big increase in the price of petrol would not lead to a quick switch to energy efficient public transport, because it would take too long to re-build the public transport infrastructure. If the 'locked in' theory is right, then the relatively small changes in price that are envisaged in an eco-tax system, although beyond those required for 'efficiency', would still not have the desired environmental outcome. There is some truth in this argument, although care must be taken to consider the issues concretely and in context.

A more important objection to eco-taxes is related to the question of fair distribution. Carbon taxes are regressive, since the poor spend a greater proportion of their income on energy. The high tax rates that would be needed to have a chance of making an environmental impact would exacerbate this uneven distribution. Also, if such high rates were contemplated, it would hit the profits of big business and make them politically impossible to impose. It is significant that in Scandinavian countries where some form of eco-tax was implemented in the 1990s, companies were specifically excluded from paying, and the whole burden was put on individuals.

3.2 Constraints on capitalism

All the capitalist theories to achieve sustainability: property rights, tradable permits or eco-taxes, remain just that - theories. The reasons why none of them have ever been implemented in a manner to seriously address global warming are much more important than the individual criticisms that can be made of each. The thinking elements of the capitalist classes internationally realise that an abyss is looming, so why can they not take really decisive action?

The issue should be absolutely clear: the long-term costs of global warming, as the Stern report into its economic effects spelled out, far exceed the immediate costs of mitigation, so why have the capitalists found it so hard to come to an agreement? For example, why can't the British government emulate its predecessor in the 19th Century which took action on the environment, when the irresponsible actions of individual firms threatened the prospects of the system as a whole? Then, the Prime Minister, Disraeli, introduced several pieces of legislation. These included the Rivers Pollution Act of 1876 and the Sale of Food and Drugs Act of 1874. The Rivers

Pollution Act prohibited the introduction of solid waste into rivers, preventing further pollution by sewage and made manufacturers liable to render harmless liquids flowing from their works. The Sale of Food and Drugs Act attempted to prevent the adulteration of food by unscrupulous suppliers. To answer the question of why the representatives of capitalism today cannot repeat the action of their forebears in tackling environmental problems goes to the heart of the dilemma they face.

'Tory leader Cameron pretended to be green in opposition and then slashed spending on the environment when in power

The Stranglehold of Imperialism

It was much easier in the mid-19th century for Disraeli to take action to tackle environmental pollution because the problem was restricted largely within national boundaries. Further, the antagonisms between countries over trade, and the profits resulting from it, are far greater now, in an imperialist age, than they were then when Britain was the dominant world power and did not need to worry so much about her international rivals (see box on Imperialism). Since the end of the 19th Century, capitalism has become a world system characterised initially by a massive expansion in the trade of goods, then by the export of capital on a huge scale, as analysed by Lenin,[9] and finally by the 'export' of production through the agency of competing multinational corporations. Despite these manifestations of globalisation, the nation-state simultaneously has grown in importance as the defender, by force ultimately, of the monopolies that lie under its jurisdiction, as competition for profit between firms based in different countries has intensified. This contradiction, between the needs of individual capitalists to push down national barriers in the quest for profit and their continued reliance on the nation state to defend their vital interests, is undiminished today. It led to the wars and horrors of the 20th Century and makes the international agreement that is necessary to reverse global warming a remote possibility.

Lenin, the leader of the Russian Revolution of 1917, analysed the antagonisms between the main capitalist powers in his pamphlet *Imperialism-the highest stage of capitalism*

Imperialism

Imperialism is a concept that is used here to help explain the factors preventing meaningful agreement being reached to combat global warming. Since the word 'imperialism' is found in a variety of contexts, where it is given different meanings, and because the concept is central to many of the arguments deployed, its use in this book is explained below.

Imperialism is not used here to describe the political and economic systems of the empires of the ancient world, nor is it used for those of the 18th and 19th Century, that were based on the conquest of colonies, principally by Britain and France. Rather, the definition dates from the early 20th Century and in particular Lenin's analysis of the phenomenon. VI Lenin, the leader of the Russian Revolution of 1917, wrote the pamphlet *Imperialism, the Highest Stage of Capitalism* during the First World War to explain the cause of the conflict as being rooted in modern capitalism and to expose the role of those workers' leaders who had supported their 'own' governments in the slaughter.

The underlying contradictions of capitalism that created imperialism, shown by the deep economic crises of the late nineteenth and early twentieth century, were not dealt with in Lenin's short book, rather they were implied. He never intended his work to be the last word on the subject, not least since, as he commented in the introduction to the 1920 edition, the original was written under the censorship then operating. This meant more overtly political issues could not be raised. Bearing this last point in mind, it is important not to try to reduce imperialism to a purely economic phenomenon, or to assume there is a simple cause and effect linking economic and political factors.

As a shorthand definition, Lenin dubbed imperialism 'monopoly capitalism' and followed this up with an analysis of five particular features that characterised the imperialist epoch: the concentration of capital, the merging of finance and industrial capital, the export of capital over and above commodities, the development of cartels internationally and finally the territorial re-division of the world by the big powers by force of arms. All these features were driven by the need of Capital to find profitable outlets, which, as the 19th century progressed, found itself increasingly constrained by national boundaries, but unable to break through them. This was because capitalism historically developed inside the framework of the nation state and every capitalist class remained ultimately dependant on the location where its wealth was based.

A national consciousness developed in each country, based on culture and history, and usually reinforced by a common language. These factors created huge obstacles to the market system breaking out of its national shackles - a reality that persists today. At the beginning of the 20th Century, despite the historical constraints, capital nevertheless had to continue to try to exploit new markets by expanding beyond national borders, leading to conflict with competitors from other countries, and ultimately to war.

Lenin's first four points above are still clearly relevant today, albeit with some modification. The concentration of capital has proceeded to levels undreamed of in the early 20th century, recent research has shown that 147 corporations, operating through extensive networks of interconnected firms, control 40% of the world's wealth.[10] Also, although cartels are now mostly formally outlawed (the oil producers cartel, OPEC, being an exception), monopolisation means that it has never been easier for collusion to take place by multinational corporations in their quest to rig and dominate markets.

Another of Lenin's points, the coming together of industrial and finance capital, has continued in a variety of ways, with finance becoming increasingly dominant. For example, it has been estimated that by 1999, 20% of employment in London and New York was in the finance sector, a figure that has certainly increased since.[11] The export of commodities, and then increasingly of capital, described by Lenin, has been followed by a further international expansion of capital in the form of production, as multinational corporations have established operations throughout the globe.

The final point in Lenin's summary of the key features of imperialism, the re-division of the world market between the main industrialised powers by force of arms, did though appear to have been superseded by a new historical reality after 1945. The 2nd World War marked the last time there was an imperialist war, where the protagonists were the main capitalist powers, principally, Britain, Germany, France, Japan and the USA. (The war remained imperialist between these powers, even after the scenario was complicated when the non-capitalist Soviet Union was involved in the conflict.) However, after WW2, the balance in international relations was profoundly altered when the clear victors emerged as the USSR and the USA. The capitalist classes had then to cooperate to present a united front in the Cold War struggle with the Soviet Union, whose alternative, non-capitalist social system, although a caricature of real socialism, nevertheless represented a serious threat to all the main imperialist powers.

Building a united front was made simpler by two key factors. The first was the domination of the USA over the other big capitalist nations, enabling it to an extent to dictate the political agenda. The second was the economic 'golden age' of 1950-75, that helped mask the continuing underlying conflicts of interests between the powers. The West European countries were also prepared to sacrifice some sovereignty to the EU, in order to try to challenge the economic hegemony of the USA.

Although confrontation and tension between the main capitalist governments remained, and nation states continued to protect the interests of firms based within their territory, co-operation was nevertheless a significant feature of the post war period. The reasons for the temporary change in the balance between confrontation and cooperation were due to the new circumstances, not to any change in the predatory nature of capitalism.[12]

Today, the conjuncture of factors that forced cooperation on the capitalists is breaking down rapidly. Key turning points were the collapse of the USSR in 1991 and the onset, in 2008 of (in the words of the Governor of the Bank of England) 'the worst financial crisis in history', that decisively and finally consigned the 'golden age' to history. Confrontation is again becoming predominant, with new evidence continually emerging of conflicts between the main industrialised nations, such as the crisis in the EU and the total impasse in the WTO sponsored international trade negotiations. Despite these clashes, armed conflict between the main powers is not on the agenda, at least in the short or medium term. This is due to the huge inherent dangers to the capitalists of going down this road, as well as to the continuing military dominance of the USA. The failure of attempts to address climate change, that stretched over 20 years, was a harbinger of the move away from post-war cooperation. As has been pointed out already, the costs of taking action were relatively small, but the growing economic and political tensions between the principal capitalist countries prevented agreement.

The 147 multinational companies that control 40% of the world's wealth and dominate the world economy resist fiercely anything that could threaten their profits in the short term, even to a small extent, and look to their 'home' countries to assist them in doing this. This is particularly true of US corporations, because the USA accounts for over 20% of all greenhouse gas output. Its firms would stand to lose far more than key rivals in Europe or Japan from any effective action to reduce global warming that 'made the polluter pay'.

There is some truth in the Stern report when it says that if the costs were spread over 45 years they should be manageable, the figure given is 1% of world GDP per year. (This figure is probably an underestimate since it ignores, among other factors, the likelihood that world temperatures will rise much more sharply and sooner than current models predict, due to so-called feedback effects.) Nevertheless, even if the costs are two or even three times greater, they should be manageable in terms of the overall cost to society. This cuts no ice with the US Congress though, even if the effects on profits could be relatively small if spread over decades. It has refused to engage in any meaningful process that could lead to an obligation to cut emissions. (It is significant that it was Clinton and his 'green' Vice-President Al Gore who vetoed participation in the Kyoto process, because it was seen as the thin end of the wedge, even if it did prove to be almost completely ineffective.)

Montreal Protocol

Could this US intransigence change in the future - because without American participation any international agreement would be virtually worthless? After all, the evidence is now irrefutable that a major threat is looming. The experience of Hurricane Katrina should have brought home the domestic costs of global warming. Also, there is a precedent for the USA to participate in international action to tackle environmental pollution, when it reached agreement in the late 1980s under UN auspices, to cut out the use of CFC chemicals in aerosols sprays. They were causing the breakdown of the ozone layer in the upper atmosphere, which lead to an increased risk of skin cancer for large sections of the world's population.

The Montreal protocol was quite effective in reducing CFC levels, which fell by 77% percent between 1988 and 1994, so could this be a model for future action on climate change, as many environmentalists think? There are some crucial differences though between the two that have to be considered. Firstly, the scale of the problem is entirely different, because the cost of eliminating a single chemical from a production process, when substitutes were already available, was insignificant compared to ultimately replacing the world's entire energy generating capacity. Second, the cost of removing CFCs affected all the industrialised capitalist countries on a roughly even

Planning for the Planet: How Socialism Could Save the Enviroment

basis, when GDP per capita was considered. (Even so, the USA delayed for years before ratifying the Montreal agreement, and only did so when one of its chemical corporations, DuPont Inc., made a technical breakthrough, enabling it to dominate the CFC substitute market.)

In the case of greenhouse gas emissions, the USA is one of the biggest polluters in absolute terms, as it was with CFCs. However, in contrast to the other polluters it accounts for 20% of emissions with only 5% of the world's population, i.e. its per capita consumption is four times the world average, and nearly twice the EU emissions per head. Therefore if the polluter pays proportionately, as the other industrialised countries insist, the USA will be in by far the worst position. This will make it very difficult for a future US president who wanted to take action on global warming to use the example of CFCs to support her or his case.

China

Another objection the US multinationals always raise with regard to action on global warming is the position of China. China along with all other ex-colonial and third world countries was not expected to participate in the Kyoto process in the early 1990s, because its output (particularly per head) of pollutants was very small compared to the imperialist countries. Now however the situation has changed in China, which

China is now the biggest emitter of greenhouse gases. The World Health Organisation has estimated that the country's industrial emissions have created seven of the world's ten most polluted cities

has the largest environmental footprint. The USA insists that any future agreements on global warming must include China, which is a major strategic rival. China, quite understandably, responds by pointing out that the current problem was caused almost entirely by the imperialist countries, and it should not be penalised as a result.

The opposition by the US multinationals to giving what they will characterise as a free-ride to their main emerging strategic rival will be a major obstacle to reaching any worthwhile agreement on global warming. The US bosses also realise that even if the Chinese government does sign up to an international agreement to cut greenhouse gases, its ability to make it work is limited. At the moment, China has some environmental legislation as rigorous as in the West, but it is largely ignored on the ground. The wild-west nature of the development of capitalism in China has meant that local bureaucrats and capitalists have operated independently of the central government in many areas and have ignored inconvenient environmental laws passed in Beijing, almost with impunity. Despite more recent attempts to promote energy efficiency, China will remain the biggest emitter of greenhouse gases as long as her economy continues to expand on a market basis. Like the USA, China will evade serious action on climate change if profits are threatened, whether in or out of any future cap and trade scheme.

3.2.1 Direct state intervention

Direct state intervention to reduce pollution, although still operating within the framework of a market driven society, has been largely discarded as an option by the currently dominant neo-liberal alchemists, who dismissively label it 'command and control'. Some pro-capitalist commentators though are beginning to reconsider this attitude, because they think direct intervention may actually work, in contrast to neo-liberal theorising. A strategy that they propose is to impose a legally enforceable set of standards to control emissions. Other options could also include more radical measures. For instance, action to redirect production to non-polluting sectors, to restrict consumer choice to eco-friendly products or to prescribe that energy be produced by renewable sources.

As the environmental crisis deepens, the attractiveness of this approach will grow, particularly to those on the left or active in the green movement who can see the impotence of purely market based ideas. Although state intervention could have an effect if it was applied in all the major polluting countries in a large-scale manner over the long-term, the question is - will it be? It is possible that an individual country will begin to implement small-scale environment-friendly measures, such as in Germany or in a Scandinavian state. However, as soon as the level of investment by the state threatens profits through higher taxes, as it must if the measures are to be sufficiently large scale to be effective, the big companies will scream that their international competitiveness is being undermined. Since in the context of capitalism, the priority of each country's government is to protect the interests of the multinational companies based inside their borders, any meaningful environmental programme would then be resisted, or be implemented at a minimal and consequently ineffective level. The requirement to solve the crisis, which is to have international agreements capable of tackling the scale of the problem, remains the same, as do the reasons why agreement has proved elusive.

3.2.2 The lessons of the Copenhagen Summit

Even more than the Durban UN climate conference of 2011, the failure of its predecessor in Copenhagen in 2009, which was meant to fix the failings of the Kyoto system, demonstrates graphically the points made above about the inability of the capitalist class to tackle global warming. Analysing the detail of Copenhagen events, a meeting that the UN in advance had called 'the last chance to avoid catastrophic global warming', reveals the contradictions lying at the heart of imperialism. One of the chief mouthpieces of finance capital expressed the failure in the starkest terms. Condemning the 'Dismal outcome at Copenhagen fiasco', the leading article in the *Financial Times* (21/12/09) stated, '…One wonders how a conference to conclude two years of detailed negotiations, building on more than a decade of previous talks, could have collapsed into such a shambles' and further, '…Governments need to understand…that Copenhagen was worse than useless'.

Judging by the reaction of the FT, the more far-sighted representatives of the bourgeoisie were alarmed by the Copenhagen impasse, since the big industrial countries by then had accepted the reality of global warming and some had already made attempts to address the problem. However, from the start of international discussions on climate change in the early 1990s, the policy of all the main powers was to reject a so-called 'command and control' approach, advocated by some environmental campaigners. This approach argued for a ceiling to be fixed for emissions by a certain date, which would then be enforced by sanctions under criminal law. Instead negotiations began under UN auspices on a 'make the polluter pay' mechanism, incorporating a market trading system in permits to pollute, known as 'cap and trade'. This approach was embedded in the Kyoto treaty and was the basis for its intended successor at Copenhagen.

The most controversial issues were: the role and nature of participation of the USA in a new treaty, the help that would be given to 'developing' countries to reduce greenhouse gases and the level and timing of the cuts needed in carbon dioxide emissions. Another key question was the type and extent of so-called offsetting arrangements that would be permitted, i.e. where firms in industrialised countries are allowed to pollute more in return for sponsoring green projects in poor nations. To understand what the prospects were of overcoming these sticking points, some of the background to the controversies surrounding the Copenhagen talks needs first to be considered.

After nearly 10 years of argument, agreement was reached in 1997 that Kyoto would be a system of carbon permit trading that also included legally enforceable limits on carbon dioxide emissions. Each country had its own permitted level of emissions in the treaty, and within countries, firms had their own target that could only be exceeded if they bought a permit to pollute. The cost of the permit was supposed to be set at a sufficiently high level to deter firms from exceeding their quotas. The outcome of Kyoto was a total failure, in that it was unable to stop an inexorable rise in greenhouse gas emissions and a rapidly deteriorating environmental situation, in particular the melting of the polar ice caps at an unprecedented rate. The failure was due to two underlying factors, a flawed market trading model and the lack of international agreement on a variety of issues linked to the operation of the treaty, most crucially the refusal to participate of the two main carbon-emitting countries, the USA and China. Without their involvement any market in carbon permits was always going to be fundamentally undermined.

The USA refused to participate even though the Kyoto targets were extremely modest, based on a small reduction in emissions compared to 1990 levels. This date was set deliberately, since it pre-dated the economic collapse of the USSR and the subsequent big fall in greenhouse gases linked to that disaster. Consequently, virtually no actual reductions from the level of carbon dioxide output in 1997, when the treaty was signed, were required, since there had already been a large fall compared to 1990. In addition to this, numerous loopholes were built into Kyoto, such as the possibility for firms to exploit 'offsetting' arrangement scams and the propensity of governments to issue so many pollution trading permits that they became virtually worthless and therefore no deterrent. In fact, Kyoto was designed to be largely cosmetic in the hope that America would be persuaded to join, but it totally failed in this ambition as well.

An agreement at Copenhagen was supposed to address the obvious limitations of Kyoto and to ensure continuity when that treaty expired in 2012. Hopes were high in 2008 when Barack Obama was elected, which, combined with the ever more explicit and unequivocal warnings from science, would, it was hoped, give a final boost to international efforts for a breakthrough. To see what went wrong it is necessary to look in detail at the controversial issues surrounding the talks, highlighted above.

Participation of the USA

Even if America was not formally included in a treaty, all the main powers realised that the inclusion of the USA in any new arrangements was vital. Beforehand, Obama's administration consistently talked up the possibility not only of active participation in a carbon trading system, but of refusing to countenance any fudging of the rules to create loopholes, or of participating in a cosmetic exercise. This rhetoric was exposed as empty, as an interview in *New Scientist* magazine with President Obama's science advisor, John Holdren revealed. First, the level of emissions cuts the US was proposing for itself was for a reduction by 2020 to 17% below 2005 levels. This would have amounted to a few percent below 1990 emissions, i.e. less then was required under Kyoto, and delivered eight years later, since the Kyoto end date was 2012. Also, the Kyoto targets were extremely modest and largely cosmetic for reasons already discussed. But secondly, and more importantly as Holdren admitted, even this minimal package had no chance of going through the US Senate. According to his calculation, they were 12 to 15 votes short of getting the 60 needed to put the legislation through.

The help to be given to 'developing' countries to cut emissions

The Chinese government said that rich countries should pay $400bn per year, or approximately 1% of GDP, to help poor countries to cut emissions to the level needed. This compared to Britain's 'offer' of $100bn and the EU's endorsement of a $150bn figure. Within this sum, there was no agreement on dividing up the pain. Germany said that the EU should contribute $50bn, with most of the rest coming, by implication, from the USA. Within the proposed EU contribution, there was deadlock on who should pay what, which did not bode well for a wider global deal. All the EU offers, anyway, were conditional on broader agreement being reached. So, the European governments were free to posture as green champions, since they were perfectly aware that the US Senate would almost certainly refuse to endorse any agreement.

The Chinese and Indian leaders claimed, with some justification, that the problem was largely created by the industrialised capitalist countries. Their emissions were five (China) and ten (India) times less than for example, the UK, on a per-head basis, - so why should they pay? However, the USA had always made it clear that unless China, in particular, agreed to bear a 'fair' share of the burden, the US would not take part in any international system to reduce greenhouse gases. When the Democrats were elected in November 2008, Obama asked John Kerry, a leading Senator, to represent him at UN climate talks in Poland, designed to pave the way to Copenhagen. Many expected, given the green rhetoric coming from the Obama camp before its victory, that their position would change. But Kerry just reiterated the previous line of former President Bush. This dealt a huge blow to any hope of success, since China and India had always been adamant that they would not commit to any target for greenhouse gas reductions. China had agreed only to cut her carbon intensity, i.e. emissions per unit of GDP, and by an unspecified amount. Since China's economy was growing rapidly, this would mean that greenhouse gas output would continue to rise despite any improvements in energy efficiency. Poor countries would only have committed themselves to meaningful targeted cuts was if significant money was on the table from the industrialised world, and there was no prospect of this. In the meantime, since China was the biggest global emitter of carbon dioxide any international agreement excluding it would have a limited impact.

The level and timing of cuts in carbon dioxide emissions.

This issue was at the heart of the climate negotiations. Most industrialised states had agreed to a cut of 80% in emissions by 2050, the level generally agreed necessary to eventually stabilise global temperatures. Since the implementation date was sufficiently far away to be ignored by capitalist politicians, no concrete measures were put in place to address this target. However, the Intergovernmental Panel on Climate Change (IPCC) was also saying that to have even a 50% chance of avoiding a temperature rise of 2 degrees there had to be a 25-40% reduction in emissions by 2020 in industrialised countries. A corresponding 15-30% reduction in 'developing' countries was also needed. If temperatures went above this level there would be a bigger danger of 'tipping effects' occurring that can lead to run-away warming.

Two years earlier at the Bali summit to prepare the ground for Copenhagen, it was agreed that the IPCC figure for 2020 should guide the target setting for industrialised countries. After Bali most big developed nations (except the EU) had, at meeting after meeting, refused to turn this into concrete emissions targets at either an aggregate or individual country level. As a result the offers on the table amounted to a reduction of only 10-17% below 1990 levels. The EU had made a 'generous' offer to cut 20%, but strictly on condition that agreement was reached in Copenhagen. Its position was part of a cynical game, since it knew the chances of the USA agreeing to significant cuts were minimal, which would then allow the Europeans to take their offer off the table. In fact, as discussed earlier, America was proposing to cut only a few percentage points below 1990 levels, and the likelihood of even this tiny cut being agreed by the US Senate was remote. As far as poorer countries were concerned, the key nations, China and India, categorically refused to set any targets to reduce carbon dioxide output.

The type and extent of offsetting arrangements

Offsetting was a system where rich countries could avoid meeting their emissions targets by agreeing to fund green projects in poor countries. It was one of the main reasons the Kyoto treaty was totally ineffective, since there was enormous scope for fudging, misreporting and corruption. According to Friends of the Earth, it seems that the Copenhagen offsetting rules would permit funding for poor countries to build coal fired power stations, despite being the worst culprits for CO_2 emissions. They would only have to have been slightly more energy efficient than the ones they replaced. Even if offsetting projects were genuine, the approach would still be flawed since the IPCC had clearly said that greenhouse gases must be cut massively in both industrialised and poor countries, an aim offsetting undermined.

Rather than accepting this, the EU was planning to offset half of its emissions target proposed for Copenhagen. If Copenhagen had been successful and its target implemented, the EU would have had to reduce its carbon dioxide production by only 10% after allowing for offsetting. This puts the apparently generous European Union offer into perspective. Also, if offsetting was implemented, it would reduce the pressure in the EU to convert to sustainable energy production methods, and in the process to create green jobs, which is the only effective way to tackle global warming.

A particularly cynical form of offsetting proposed at Copenhagen was to allow rich nations to buy forest carbon credits, i.e. including the forests in a cap and trade scheme. Industrialised countries would buy large areas of rainforests, preventing further clearances because of the new owners' more responsible attitude. Apart from producing gales of laughter, this rationale, pushed in particular by the UK, had all the general drawbacks of offsetting plus some extra pernicious elements. For example, the

Offsetting proposals in UN climate talks would have had terrible effects on the indigenous peoples of the Amazon'

system included agricultural plantations in the definition of 'rainforest', meaning that funding from rainforest offsetting could have been used to continue to clear the forests and replace them with agricultural land. The problem is that plantations only absorb 20% as much CO_2 as forests, so making a mockery of the whole process. (Rainforests are important in fighting climate change because 10% of all greenhouse gas emissions are a result of deforestation, since trees absorb large amounts of carbon dioxide). The forest offsetting proposal would also have had terrible effects on the indigenous peoples of these regions, with land grabs and violent evictions occurring as the forests continued to be cleared, to be replaced with 'agricultural plantations'.

3.3 The green movement agenda for tackling the environmental crisis

The culpability of imperialism, blamed here for the developing environmental catastrophe, is also accepted by many if not most green activists. But do the various eco-alternatives to the current form of capitalism, which is competing multinational corporations defended by nation states, really offer a way to tackle the crisis? There are many variations of the Green and environmental movement agenda, so any categorisation must be approximate and recognise that there is overlap between them. Bearing this in mind, it is still possible to identify three basic trends or approaches. The first two are models based on market solutions, albeit with significant state involvement, that are considered below. The third is sometimes called eco-socialist, where market forces are not the dominating feature, which will be discussed in Chapter 6.

The 'mainstream' market approach asserts the central need for a steady state economy. Steady state was defined by its initial proponent and guru of the movement, Hermann Daly, as fixing absolute limits both to human population and to the 'population' of artefacts (goods).[10] The question of population control is controversial, and will be discussed in Chapter 6, but putting a limit to the production of goods is a common feature of most green policies. The programme of the Green Party in Britain includes: import/export controls, control on multinationals through exchange controls, control on speculation through the 'Tobin tax', limits on the size of monopolies and tax breaks for new small firms entering the market. At the centre of the programme is a complex system of eco-taxes and permits to encourage environmentally friendly behaviour which, it is claimed, will lay the basis for a steady state economy.

What would be the implications of a steady state economy? If steady state is defined as zero consumption growth from present levels, a 66% reduction in carbon intensity would be needed to tackle global warming. (Intensity is defined here as output of pollution per unit of consumption. e.g. the amount of CO_2 produced in making a tonne of steel). This assumes the widely predicted large population increase in the global 'South' and a small one in the 'North'. (See the appendix for details of this calculation which is derived from the so-called Commoner-Erlich equation.) However, if it is true, as most Greens believe, that this level of reduction in environmental intensity is not feasible, then consumption will have to fall to close the gap.

If consumption must decline, what implications does this have for the Green programme to redistribute the 'surplus' from the North to the South to establish a fair and equal world? If we assume, on the grounds of fairness and equality, that cuts are limited to the main polluters in the industrialised countries, consumption per head will have to be reduced significantly. In these circumstances the scope for redistributing the industrialised countries' 'surplus' consumption to the rest of the world would be very limited, since it would have shrunk enormously. This is true with steady state defined as meaning zero consumption growth. Most Greens advocate a cut in consumption, which would reduce the surplus even further.

The Greens correctly make the point that definitions of consumption are based on GDP (Gross Domestic Product) calculations that are boosted by the costs of clearing up environmental damage. The argument goes that since growth in GDP is a policy objective of all governments there is no incentive to cut pollution, because the pollution itself is contributing to GDP growth. The conclusion made by the Greens is that if the definition of GDP is changed to eliminate this effect, governments will change growth policy in an environmentally friendly way. Apart from the technical difficulties in doing this, the reasoning assumes that government policy can fundamentally control economic growth.

Capitalist states all have a desire for growth, since growth boosts both the profits of the corporations they ultimately represent and their own power and prestige. But making desire become reality is not so easy, because the market system is out of the control of any firm, however big, or country, even the USA. Since the system has its own internal logic based on the international competition for markets and the quest for profit, individual governments can affect what happens only to a small extent. This was graphically shown by the financial crisis of 2008. However, the question of compensating for the 'polluting' effect of growth projections will need to be addressed when society really is in control of the economy, i.e. in a non-capitalist system.

Socialists and Greens agree that the exploitation of the environment is linked directly to the activities of the monopoly corporations, 147 of which dominate the world economy. Is the answer, as the Greens claim, to go back to societies where small local firms operate in a steady state market system? Leaving aside the impossibility of turning back the wheel of history in this way, if such a system was created, the fundamental law of the market would still apply, i.e. a need for continuous growth and an unlimited increase in production. This is because the capitalist market is anonymous and dominated by the laws of competition. Each industrialist tries to grab as large a share of the market as possible, but to do this requires cutting prices without threatening profit. The only way to achieve this is to reduce the cost of production by cutting the value of commodities, via reducing the labour time necessary to produce them, in order to produce more commodities in the same length of time. To bring about such an increase in production, capital must be invested to rationalise the labour process, and the only source of this capital, in the final analysis, is profit. In other words, the dynamic of the system is the constant accumulation of capital, driven by competition, and paid for by the surplus value (profit) produced in the course of production itself. This feature of the capitalist economy, analysed by Marx,[14] fundamentally undermines the proponents of the small, steady state market economy. The absolute need will always be there for it to grow and break out of any controls on economic expansion that might be imposed by a green government. In such circumstances, monopolies would eventually emerge, as Marx predicted they would when analysing the dynamics of growth of pre-monopoly capitalism in the nineteenth century.

The green macro-economic programme is based on limiting the operation of the market internationally through exchange controls, limiting capital flows and speculation and imposing import-export controls. Despite the internationalist

Marx analysed the need of the capitalist system for the constant accumulation of capital

outlook of most Greens, this programme points in the opposite direction, towards a siege economy which will foster national prejudices and preclude the international co-operation needed for sustainability. Also, the plank of the Green programme to ensure international co-operation, i.e. imposing tariffs on countries refusing to implement environmentally friendly policies, would lead to conflict. The USA has the most to lose, since it is, with China, the biggest polluter, and it would use its dominance to punish any international trade body or country that attempted to go down this path.

It might be argued that the large degree of state control necessary for a siege economy could lead to the establishment of a steady state environmentally friendly society, albeit only on a national basis. However, even if a government went a long way down the road of state control, if the market remained, the growth dynamic would eventually reassert itself. In these circumstances, if the state continued to stand in the way of expansion and profits, conflict would be inevitable. During the Labour government in Britain in the 1970s, there was ferocious resistance by the capitalists, including the plotting of a coup by some elements, when the Prime Minister, Wilson, took half a step in the direction of a programme that had some similarities to that of the Greens. In the end, a 'Green' government would either have to capitulate to the demands of the market or move to abolish it. Even if an eco-capitalist siege economy could maintain itself for a period, the measures in the Green programme to reduce pollution, based on market mechanisms such as eco-taxes and permits, would be inadequate. They would also lead to more inequality, contrary to the stated aims of the Greens, since eco-taxes hit the poorest hardest.

The Green Growth Agenda

A second strand of Green thinking supports the concept of green growth, rather than advocating steady state or cuts in consumption. Most serious advocates of green growth, who want to address poverty in the 'South' as well as tackling global warming, say that it is possible to reduce carbon intensity sufficiently to allow the sustainable expansion of consumption using market methods, although not necessarily those of neo-classical economics. The problems with such a programme were analysed earlier, where the conclusion was reached that the market tools available, such as eco-taxes, are inadequate for the scale of the task. This would particularly be the case if significant growth in the global South was allowed for, which would need carbon intensity to be reduced by over 90%. (see Appendix). More significantly, the introduction of carbon taxes would reduce the profits of the multinationals, particularly in the USA, and would therefore be strongly opposed. Even if the tax hikes were relatively small, the lesson of the collapse of the Copenhagen summit is that any concession in this direction is fiercely resisted by all the imperialist powers and China. Market-based green growth advocates also put significant emphasis on the possibilities of new technology, which is discussed briefly later.

Green Keynesianism

A new tendency in the green growth movement, emerging since the 2008 crisis and whose programme raises important issues, is Green Keynesianism. This approach eschews micro supply-side measures and instead puts forward radical action by the state to tackle environmental problems and unemployment simultaneously. It is true that despite the extreme reluctance of nation states and the big corporations they represent, to pay for meaningful action (or as it is increasingly becoming evident from Copenhagen and Durban, any action to tackle climate change), governments nevertheless must be pressurised by the labour movement and environmental activists into spending the money needed to address the issue. This does, though, pose the important questions of to what extent the reluctance of capitalist society to take climate action can be overcome by sufficiently determined campaigners and trade unions, and what political lessons need to drawn from the capitalists' intransigent opposition.

To pay for a switch to renewable energy and other measures necessary to cut emissions, a combination of borrowing, printing money and taxing the rich has been put forward- a form of Green Keynesianism.[21] The point is made that it is not unprecedented in Britain for similar measures, and on an even bigger scale, to be put into practice. As well as the 2008 financial crisis, the example is given of the Second World War, where capitalist governments massively expanded spending and introduced extensive public control and planning. The key question posed by the green Keynesian argument is how can the present government be made to take similarly decisive action on climate change? Two main tactics are suggested, firstly raising awareness, particularly at work, through trade union organised interventions and secondly, action, most importantly in the workplace. Examples of action could be having campaigning union environmental reps pushing managements into introducing green measures, organising or supporting demos and ultimately strikes. It is proposed workers made redundant in the car industry could occupy their factory to demand it be converted to renewable production. If necessary, industrial action would have to be organised on a national level by more than one union.

The industrial initiatives proposed will be very important, as shown by the struggles of the Vestas wind turbine workers. (Regarding the proposed trade union initiatives, care must be taken not to slip into class-collaborationism which is a danger in the way the issue can be posed. Promoting a 're-all-in-this-together' mentality, even inadvertently, will rebound on union activists when management come back to demand sacrifices 'to save the planet'.) However, to understand the reasons behind the bosses' resistance, broader political issues need to be addressed.

Workers and their families at the Vestas wind turbine factory in the Isle of Wight protesting against the plant's closure

The Keynesian measures that have been called for will be strongly resisted, not least because in WW2 all the capitalist governments involved were fighting for their lives, whereas today none see climate change as similarly important, so the war analogy is of very limited relevance. Even though the cost of tackling global warming is relatively small, and most governments also now accept the seriousness of the situation, so far, all continue to refuse to take any serious action. This is because they don't want to hit the profits, even in a small way, of 'their' multinational companies.

Faced with very widespread strikes, the bourgeoisie can be forced to back down, but the capitalists would soon try to reverse any concessions, in order to reassert their short-term economic interests. The most likely scenario in which decisive change is achieved would be if environmental struggles are linked to a broader movement of the Trade Unions, provoked by direct attacks on the working class, as in the 1926 General Strike. This would inevitably then pose the issue of capitalism or socialism. In this sense, if socialism was victorious, reversing global warming would be a by-product of the class struggle, in some way similar to how a socialist transformation would have achieved 'world peace' in the 1930s, as Leon Trotsky explained at the time.

If they were attempted, the Keynesian economic methods that have been proposed, such as printing and borrowing money and taxing the rich (the last to be welcomed of course), would also provoke huge opposition from the ruling class. At the very least, the markets would demand savage cuts in other areas to pay for a climate intervention. They would not, as after WW2, allow 60 years to pay off the debt, which was permitted at that time due to the more favourable economic climate of the post-war boom and the political requirements to tread softly due to the Cold War. Even so, paying off the post-WW2 Marshall Plan debt entailed austerity and rationing.

Now, if a government baulked at the cuts demanded there would be a run on the currency and the spectre of having to put up interest rates sharply to defend it, or face runaway inflation, either way leading at some point to a future bust. Printing money would have a similar effect in causing a run on the pound, as the markets anticipated their Sterling investments being eroded by higher inflation.

It could be argued of course that market speculation could be prevented by imposing a siege economy, involving controls on capital and foreign trade. This would be resisted by British capitalism though, since it is now heavily dependent on the free international trade in financial services and the profits of speculation to balance the books. Also, imposing import controls would lead to retaliation and a repeat of the self-defeating beggar-your-neighbour policies of the 1930s, that characterised the Great Depression. The Keynesian interventions in the 1930s didn't end the Great Depression, it was only rearmament for war that eventually reduced unemployment.

3.4 New Technology

The first point that needs to be made on this issue is that the technology exists now to help tackle climate change, in the shape of wind, wave and solar power systems, high-speed rail, electric cars etc., but it has not been implemented to a significant extent because the capitalists regard it as too expensive. Is it possible though that new technology could ride to the rescue by producing green energy at low cost? This is certainly the hope of neo-liberals and some green growth supporters, although the two tendencies base their ideas on different conceptions of technological change.

The neo-liberals think that market competition will drive innovation, having the effect of raising the general level of productivity so that energy use falls for a given level of consumption. It is true that over the long-term, productivity has risen by about 2% per year in industrialised countries,[15] leading to a fall in the amount of natural resources needed for a certain level of consumption.[16] However, this decease has been accompanied by a gradual rise in the consumption of natural resources per capita, therefore not necessarily leading to any cut in pollution. This indicates that productivity gains are unable to counter the environmental results of economic growth in a capitalist context.

If the problem exists in industrialised countries with access to the latest technology, it will be far greater in the so-called emerging economies in the ex-colonial world, some of which are rapidly expanding greenhouse gas outputs. To meet emissions targets to tackle global warming, technology-led productivity gains are required to allow huge cuts in natural resource use at the same time as accommodating economic growth. There is no prospect of this under capitalism, certainly not in the short time still left to take decisive action.

Falling back to a secondary line of defence, free-marketeers also trumpet the supposed 'dynamism' of the system. They say capitalism is characterised - making a virtue out of necessity - by its disruptive and unpredictable nature, which drives radical new thinking and approaches, leading to breakthrough technologies being introduced. It is theoretically possible, of course, that the fat will be pulled out of the environmental fire by a fortuitous new invention. For example, a technology like nuclear fusion that promised to produce large quantities of energy cheaply and without pollution, but there is nothing viable on the horizon.

The market system has been unable to provide the scientific breakthroughs that are needed. One of the reasons is that under monopolised capitalism, new technology is the result of long-term incremental advances by teams of scientists and engineers working for big bureaucracies in multinational corporations, where to change course to a radically different direction is very difficult. Furthermore, the huge costs of developing the new approaches that are needed in the energy field deter most companies from entering the market. If the capitalist governments had put in the same relative resources and urgency into developing fusion power as they did for the nuclear bomb during World War Two there is a good chance they could have cracked the problem. But for the reasons analysed in the section above on Green Keynesianism they were never prepared to put the money in to do this.

Some tendencies in the environmental movement who support green growth also set great store on new technology to help achieve this. Unlike the neo-liberals, they do not advocate a pure free-market approach, rather they support more state interventionism to facilitate the introduction of new technology to meet social and environmental needs. These ideas are sometimes connected to 'win-win' theories, the basis of which is that firms are unaware of the possibilities that new technologies and process innovations (i.e. new organisational methods) can provide to both tackle the environment and to make profits. It is the job of government to foster institutions and introduce regulations, containing elements of carrot and stick, to encourage the bosses to pick this 'low-hanging fruit'.

Although there is not the space here to analyse these theories in any detail, they ultimately run up against the logic of capitalism. Since the lure of profit is still ultimately the reason for investment in new technology in a competitive market, it will be introduced in those sectors that are most profitable in the short and medium term, i.e. for fossil fuel technology rather than renewable energy generation. The former New Labour government were strong supporters of the institutionalist theory outlined above, but only in words. As soon as they realised that implementing it would go against the grain of the profit system, even to a limited extent, it was largely dropped.

3.5 The way forward

Even if the scheme proposed at Copenhagen had been agreed and then implemented without any backsliding by all the key players, including the USA and China, and with all the loopholes removed, cap and trade would still have been a flawed mechanism to prevent global temperatures from rising more than 2C. The scale of the cuts needed and the relatively short time available means that any method that relied on constructing market disincentives to pollute would be inadequate. At best, the impact of this approach would have been gradual. It would have reduced global emissions at far too slow a rate to meet the need identified by climate science to cut emissions by 40% by 2020, which is required to keep temperature rises to below 2C. Even the strongest supporters of cap and trade never envisaged that it could deliver change at anything like this rate.

Carbon Taxes

It is true that directly applied carbon taxes, that produced, for example, a doubling of fuel prices, would have a bigger impact than cap and trade on greenhouse gas output. Leaving aside for the moment questions of fairness, there would though still be limitations to the effectiveness of such a policy. Relying on the operation of price signals in this way, in a largely monopolised energy market, would have a relatively small impact as has been discussed already. Any eventual change that relied on carbon taxes would anyway also be partly dependent on the money raised being spent on global warming mitigation. This would be far from certain, since capitalist governments have consistently shown they have other priorities.

What carbon taxes would do though, especially if they were implemented on a scale intended to have a serious impact on emissions, would be to hit the poorest sections of society, since the poor spend a greater proportion of their incomes on fuel. Any such regressive measures should therefore be opposed by socialists. It is true that consumer behaviour can be sensitive to price- for example in the choice between private and public transport. But a subsidy to the latter, designed to cut both fares and boost capacity, would have a more positive effect on environmental behaviour than a tax rise on fuel and would benefit the poor, rather than penalise them. This was shown by the experience in London in the 1980s, when the then Greater London Council with a left leadership slashed public transport fares.

Seeing the urgency of the situation, many activists are now calling for non - market, direct measures to be implemented to reduce greenhouse gases. Laws would be introduced to establish a ceiling in emissions by a certain date, and any transgression would then be dealt with using criminal sanctions. It is true that if an appropriate emissions level was set and then enforced rigorously on an international scale, it could make serious inroads into the climate change problem. However, if the bourgeoisies of the main polluting states opposed the largely cosmetic measures proposed at Durban and Copenhagen, any new approach with real teeth would meet with even more determined resistance.

The evidence is now overwhelming that despite their fine words, the ruling classes, in Britain and internationally, do not want to take any meaningful action to tackle climate change in the foreseeable future. Indeed, the financial and economic crisis that began in 2007 has made it likely that even token, halfhearted measures, modeled on the Kyoto treaty, will be opposed by most states. For instance, the USA resolutely refused to participate in an international treaty to reduce greenhouse gases, even when it was offered a system at Copenhagen that was full of loopholes. Environmental activists should join with the Labour Movement to fight the do-nothing policies of the capitalists. However, as well as campaigning for decisive action, political lessons must also be drawn from the 20 years that have already been lost in the battle against climate change.

Environmental activists should join with the Labour Movement to fight the do-nothing policies of the capitalists

The Nuclear Option

Like most European governments, the US is still embracing the 'lesser evil' of nuclear power as an alternative way out of the dilemma. This is despite the evidence of the 2011 nuclear disaster in Japan and that renewable energy sources become comparatively less expensive if the true long-term costs of nuclear power are included. These costs include storing ever increasing amounts of nuclear waste for tens of thousands of years, decommissioning power stations and creating a fund to deal with the effects of a Chernobyl-type disaster in the future. However, the long-term costs of nuclear power will be effectively ignored by capitalist governments, (see box on Cost Benefit Analysis), so that the profits of the multinational firms that really control the political agenda will be affected to the minimum extent.

Cost Benefit Analysis

Cost benefit analysis (CBA) is a tool that has been used to assess environmental risks and to reach a decision about future investment, by giving values to different environmental effects using a common measure, i.e. money. Costs and benefits that will fall on future generations are discounted at an agreed percentage rate, to arrive at a 'net present value'. In this way, in theory, values can be easily compared and an objective balance of costs and benefits created. Its success depends, however, on defining clearly what the costs and benefits are, and for all the parties involved to agree on these definitions. Where profit is at stake this is easier said than done.

In capitalist terms, risks must be expressed in money terms and probabilities of future adverse events clearly determined. For instance, in a CBA of global warming, the number of deaths that could result due to climate change in the future was estimated. This calculated that 22,923 would die in the advanced capitalist countries and 114,804 (both very conservative figures) in the rest of the world. The next stage in the CBA was to put a money value on these lives, which resulted in a figure of $1,480,000 per 'advanced capitalist' citizen, and $131,000 for everyone else. It is hard to see the result of this type of analysis becoming the basis of a mutual agreement based on justice and fairness.[17] When this cannot be done, which is the usual case, environmental risks are effectively ignored by using a system of ordinary discounting.

For example, using this method, it has been calculated that the cost of a nuclear accident, 500 years in the future, costing £10 billion at current prices to future generations, would be 25 pence, discounted at 5%. (using an historically typical figure). In other words, if a CBA was made now about building such a power station, 25 pence would go in the costs column to allow for a future accident. Looking at the question another way round, if a compensation fund were created now to meet the costs of this future accident, it would be necessary to invest only 25p to raise the required sum, due to workings of compound interest over such a long period. The net present cost is clearly dependent on the interest rate used, but there is no agreement on what it should be. This is not surprising since it is difficult to predict interest rates 5 months in advance, never mind 500 years. As one expert said,[18] "Through the choice of appropriate parameter values almost any (environmental) abatement policy can be justified".

Only by eliminating the power of these companies can an alternative to the nightmare scenario of environmental disaster caused by a nuclear accident or global warming become a reality.

Sustainable growth on a capitalist basis is not feasible, partly because the methods it can employ to achieve this are inadequate and flawed, but mainly because imperialist rivalry will prevent the international co-operation that is essential to make progress. The result is that the world will continue to hurtle headlong to disaster since the environment will still be treated as a 'free good' by the multinationals that dominate production and will be exploited at virtually no cost to themselves.

Appendix: The Commoner-Erlich Equations

Barry Commoner, the well known environmental writer and theorist, first developed the equation in the 70s, later modified into the form $I=P.C.T$. In this formula, I is the environmental impact, P is population, C is consumption per head and T is the environmental impact per unit of consumption. The implication of this formula, taken at face value, is that increases in personal consumption and population will increase the (negative) environmental impact. However, if T (also known as the Environmental Impact Coefficient, EIC, or environmental intensity) is reduced at the same time as P and C are going up, the negative effects of these increases can be mitigated

Calculations using the *Commoner-Erlich* Equation[19]

The equation has the form:
$I=P.C.T$
If we assume:
P^H is the population in the advanced capitalist, high income countries, P^L the equivalent figure in low income countries, C^H the consumption per head in the high income countries, C^L the consumption figure for low income areas
Then $I=[P^H.C^H + P^L.C^L] T$
If we assume P^H=902 million, C^H =$24930, P^L= 4771 million, C^L=$1090 million, therefore,
$I= [902 \times 24930+4771 \times 1090] T$

Rearranging the equation gives the current value of environmental impact per unit of consumption,

$T = I / [902.10^6 \times 24930 + 4771.10^6 \times 1090] = I/27.69 \times 10^{12}$

Now consider three cases:

1. If there is no growth in population or consumption and it is assumed that I must be reduced by 50% for sustainability, then it is clear from the equation that T must also be reduced by the same amount i.e. 50%.
2. If there is a factor of four growth in consumption per head, the population of the high income countries rises to 1186 million and the low income countries to 10160 million, and the environmental impact is reduced by 50%, then the new value of T needed for sustainability will be:
Tnew=$0.5 \times I/[1186.10^6 \times 4 \times 24930 + 10160.10^6 \times 4 \times 1090] = 0.5 \times I/162.6 \times 10^{12}$
Dividing this figure by the current estimate for T made above gives:
Tnew=$0.09 \times T$. i.e. T must be reduced by 91% for sustainability.
3. If the population rises as in example 2 above, and consumption for the entire world is 50% higher that currently found in the industrialised countries then the new value of T for sustainability will be:
Tnew=$0.5 \times I/[11346.10^6 \times 1.5 \times 24930] = I/8.5 \times 10^{14}$
Dividing this figure by the current estimate for T made above gives:
Tnew=$0.033 \times T$. i.e. T must be reduced by 97% for sustainability.

How reliable are these predictions and where did they come from?[19] Firstly, is a 50% reduction in environmental impact necessary for sustainability? The first point that needs to be made is that the *Commoner-Erlich* equation must be applied to each source of pollution separately. To aggregate the results over many disparate environmental threats would produce very arbitrary results. However, to take the example of global warming, the most serious problem of all, the Intergovernmental Panel on Climate Change (IPCC) said that CO_2 emissions need to be cut by 60% to stabilise its concentration in the atmosphere. Other greenhouse gases need to be cut by an average of more than 70% according to the IPCC. These statistics indicate therefore, that a 50% reduction in environmental impact is a conservative figure to use in predicting the conditions for sustainability due to global warming.

(A complicating factor in applying the equation is that it assumes there is no relationship between the variables of P, C and T. However, it has been claimed, using the USA as an example, that intensity in the use of resources (T) falls with rising consumption per head. This would tend to increase the cut in I needed for sustainability, compared to the case where the variables are assumed not to be related. Other examples, however, could be given which bend the results in the opposite direction. Also it is important to separate the calculations for the 'North' and the 'South', because their levels of consumption are vastly different)[20]

1 This theory was developed by Coase, in the paper: Coase, R A, 'The problem of Social Cost', *Journal of Law and Economics*, 1960, Vol, 3, 1-44
2 Environmentalist critiques of neo-classical economics can be found in *Ecological Economics. An Introduction* by Michael Common and Sigrid Stagl, published by Cambridge University Press, 2005, or in *Sustainability and Markets: on the neo-classical model of environmental economics*, by Michael Jacobs which is Chapter 4 in Planning Sustainability, edited by Michael Kenny and James Meadowcroft, Published by Routledge, London, 1999. The Common and Stagl book is handy in that it explains the arguments in some detail without the reader needing any prior knowledge of bourgeois economics. Although containing many useful and valid criticisms of neo-classical economics applied to the environment, neither publication fundamentally rejects a market-led approach, only a greater role for government than that usually advocated by neo-liberalism. For a Marxist critique of neo-classical economics see Chapter 18 of *Marxist Economic Theory* by Earnest Mandel, published by Merlin Books, 1968.
3 For the theory behind this see Chapter 9 of Common and Stagl, *op cit*.
4 These approaches are called Contingent Valuation Methods, see page 30 of Economic growth and environmental sustainability, by Paul Ekins, Routledge, London, 2000, for examples of the results they produce.
5 For example, see Chapter 2 of Ekins op cit, or Jacobs *op cit*.
6 Quoted in *The North, the South and the Environment* Edited by V Bhaskar and A Glyn, Earthscan, London, 1995. p139
7 See Jacobs *op cit*
8 See page 92 of Jacobs *op cit*
9 *Imperialism –the Highest Stage of Capitalism* by V I Lenin. Progress Publishers, Moscow, 1970
10 This research was done by a team at the Swiss Federal Institute of Technology, Zurich, who analysed a data base of 37 million companies and investors. See *New Scientist*, 22nd October 2011, p9.
11 Figures quoted by Ben Fine, in 'Examining the Ideas of Globalisation and Development Critically: What Role for Political Economy?' *New Political Economy*, Vol 9 (2), June 2004.
12 There has been controversy on the academic left over a claim that a new transnational capitalist class has emerged, linked to the emergence of transnational corporations, through whose agency Capital has finally transcended the limitations of the nation state. [see Michael Hardt and Antonio Negri, (2000), *Empire*, Cambridge, MA.: Harvard University Press]. Although the arguments cannot be taken up here, the empirical evidence does not support this theory.
13 See *Steady-State Economics*, by H E Daly, published by Earthscan, London, 1992. An eco-socialist critique of steady state is in Eco-socialism or eco-capitalism, by Saral Sarkar, Zed Books, London, 1999. For critiques from market economics, see, for example, Chapter 12 of *Principles of Environmental Economics*, by Ahmed Hussen, Routledge, London 2004.
14 Marx explains the compulsion for the capitalists to accumulate in Vol 1 of *Capital* and the mechanism behind accumulation in Chapter 21 of Volume 2 of *Capital*, Penguin Books, Harmondsworth, 1976 and 1978. Earnest Mandel covers this topic in Chapter 10 of *Marxist Economic Theory*, Merlin Books, London, 1968. See Chapter 6 of *Marx's Capital*, by Ben Fine and Alfred Saad-Filho, Pluto Press, London 2004, on the compulsion to accumulate.
15 Figure from *Capitalism Unleashed*, by Andrew Glyn, OUP, Oxford, 2006. p14.
16 see Rees, W, 'Scale, complexity and the conundrum of sustainability', in *Planning Sustainability, op. cit*.
17 Figures from Ekins, *op cit* p259
18 Fankhauser, S, 1993, 'Global Warming Economics: Issues and state of the art' CSERGE Working Paper GEC 93-28, CSERGE, University College London, London.
19 The figures are taken from Chapter 6 of Ekins, *op cit*.
20 The limitations of the Commoner-Erlich equation are dealt with by Franck Amalric in 'Population growth and the environmental crisis' in *The North, the South and the Environment. op cit*.
21 This case is put in 'One Million Climate Jobs Now!' A report by the Campaign Against Climate Change Trade Union Group for the Communication Workers Union, Public and Commercial Services Union, Rail, Maritime and Transport Union, Transport Salaried Staff Association and the University and College Union, 2009.

Chapter 4:
A Socialist Programme for the Environment

The scale and urgency of the task we face in combating the causes of global warming was shown clearly in Chapter 2. The Stern report estimated that greenhouse gases will need to be cut by up to 80% by 2050, and if the current explosive increase of emissions in China continues, by much more than this to restrict global temperature rises to 2C. In the shorter term, most climate scientists now agree that by 2020 output of polluting gases must be cut by 40% to give a chance of achieving the 2050 target.

4.1 What needs to be done?

At one level, implementing the measures needed to reach these targets is simple; no technological breakthrough is required, just the wider adoption and further development of existing technology, such as wind, wave and solar power. To tackle global warming, many environmentalists think that big cuts in consumption are needed, requiring a fundamental change in lifestyle, and deny there is a 'technical fix' of simply switching over to alternative energy sources. It is true that there is no technical fix, but the decisive factor will be changing the social system, as is argued later in the chapter, not cutting consumption. This social transformation will itself enable wind, wave and solar to be implemented on a sufficient scale to do without the need for cuts, an argument that is developed in Chapter 6. For the moment, it is enough to say that there is agreement with all Greens, in that a massive increase in the use of public transport is needed, since private transportation is such a large contributor to global warming.

The key technical elements of an approach to reduce greenhouse gas emissions are:

- Rapid conversion to the use of renewable energy sources such as wind, wave and solar power
- Big expansion of public transport

- Development of the rail network so that short and medium haul air travel can be replaced
- Conversion of car industry to using renewable energy sources
- More research into renewable energy such as clean coal technology and using materials not based on oil products

Wind and solar power is now well established and is being used more widely, but nowhere near sufficiently to meet the target of a 20% global cut in greenhouse gas emissions by 2020. Britain is lagging behind even the inadequate goals of successive governments to introduce wind power. Yet meeting targets in this country should be relatively easy, since rapid de-industrialization is removing much energy intensive industry. (Industry is of course being relocated to places like China, so just displacing the problem rather than eliminating it. This process of Western powers' 'exporting' their emissions to China has accelerated dramatically according to a report by the National Academy of Sciences (NAS) in the USA. [www.pnas.org/content/early/2011/04/19/1006388108.full.pdf] The NAS calculates that China's carbon dioxide output has increased from 4 to 7 gigatonnes in six years from 2002, overtaking the USA. Western countries' claims to be on target to meet their Kyoto commitments have to be viewed in the light of this rocketing greenhouse gas output. If the effect of this 'outsourcing' of pollution is taken into account, Britain's emissions for example, would rise by 100 million tonnes and China's would fall by a fifth.)

Wind turbines have the potential to produce several times UK annual electricity consumption

Another factor in its favour is that the UK is one of the windiest countries in the world, with potential to export a wind energy surplus. Sceptics often claim that because the wind doesn't blow all the time, it is unsuitable for energy generation since 'the lights will go out'. However, this is wide of the mark, although it is true that it would be unwise to rely on just one source of renewable energy (see box on Wind Power).

Wind Power

Ernst and Young, a consultancy company, found that Britain has the best potential in the world for off-shore wind generation due to the climate, having the possibility for 1000 terawatt hours of electricity per year, equivalent to several times annual consumption. Wind turbines use the natural power of the wind to produce electricity. The rotation of the turbine blades due to the wind drives a generator producing power that is fed into the electricity grid. A typical on-shore wind turbine is about 100m (about 300ft) tall, with blades 30-40 m long, and produces 2MW of power. This is small output compared to a conventional power station, so tens of thousands would be needed. Turbine capacity is increasing all the time as new designs come on-stream. 5MW machines already exist, so the total number required could drop rapidly. Three big wind farms, North Hoyle off the coast of North Wales, Scroby Sands near Great Yarmouth and Kentish Flats off Whitstable, are already producing electricity for the national grid.

Controversial issues are whether to develop on-shore or off-shore wind farms and whether micro-generation, e.g. each house having a wind-turbine on the roof, is a desirable option. The main benefit of on-shore development is cost, but producing off-shore electricity is inherently more efficient from a technical point of view. Wind speeds off-shore are much higher and power generated increases as a cube of wind speed, i.e. if the wind blows twice as fast, eight times as much energy is produced. Also, turbines in a wind farm need to be separated so that one machine does not take wind from another. This is often not possible in on-shore locations, because of requirements to connect to the grid and environmental concern that wind-farms are an eyesore, whose size needs to be minimised.

The problem with micro-generation is that it is less efficient than grouping turbines in wind farms because the economies of scale are lost, in particular the costs of connecting to a national grid are much higher. If such turbines are operated independently and not connected to a grid where they can be controlled centrally, the problems of intermittent operation due to variable wind speeds are much worse. (The reasons for this are discussed below.) Another drawback is that in urban areas many would think it ugly to have thousands of machines installed on roof-tops. There is also a potential problem with low-frequency noise emitted by the turbines.

The main technical objection of course to wind power, which has just been mentioned, is that when the wind does not blow no electricity can be produced. However, studies of long-term British weather patterns show that only very rarely are there still conditions over the whole country. So if turbines are positioned all round the coastline and connected to a national grid, then the problem can be minimised. This would be done by moving electricity generated where the wind is still blowing, through the grid, to the wind deficient areas. Also, the turbine itself can rotate on its own axis to catch the wind and produce power even in relatively quiet conditions.

Despite these technical measures to improve the availability of wind-generated electricity, there will always be times when other sources of energy will be needed to meet demand, particularly peak demand on a cold day. In the short-term, it would be possible to use gas-fired power stations to generate the extra power to meet the peak requirements, and still meet greenhouse gas reduction targets.

Even if there was no need to develop additional sustainable energy sources to meet peak demands, it would still be unwise to develop just one technology because of the uncertainty that has resulted from global warming itself. It is possible that patterns of ocean currents and prevailing winds in the northern hemisphere will change due to Arctic ice melting, then moving south and meeting warmer water in the Atlantic. This could disrupt the Gulf-Stream, leading to dramatic changes in the climate in north west Europe, including it becoming much less windy. It is necessary to develop some other sustainable energy sources, such as wave or tidal power, that are unlikely to be as affected by changes in ocean currents and prevailing winds.

One excuse used by government to explain why targets are not being met is the delay caused by the objections of local residents to the siting of wind-farms. It is true that they can be very noisy, and be regarded as an eye-sore. These often legitimate objections can be addressed by developing off-shore farms. Although the technology is established, wave power has not been used to any significant extent because of the high initial costs of the infrastructure, despite recent significant engineering breakthroughs making installation much simpler and potentially cheaper. Solar power use is currently expanding due to advances making solar cells more efficient and therefore useful even in cloudy regions. However, this step forward has not resulted in sufficient growth of the sector to make a significant difference to global warming. A key factor will be more research so solar generated energy can be transmitted efficiently over long distances from sunny areas.

Road transport accounts for 18% of all greenhouse gas emissions.[1] Greatly developing public transport and moving freight onto trains must therefore be an important aspect of any environmental programme, since of the 18%, the vast majority is due to cars and lorries rather than buses. This does not mean that private transportation is necessarily incompatible with reducing emissions, rather, a balance must be struck where cars are used much less and trains and buses more. A environmentally sustainable transportation sector, that includes having vehicles for personal use, will only be possible though if the car industry switches to green production. A programme to achieve this will therefore be vital and will generate green jobs (see box on Car Industry).

A Green Programme for the Car Industry

An environmentally sustainable programme for the car industry could contain the following points:

- replace existing petrol and diesel vehicles with alternatives that use electricity and hydrogen for power. Technologies exist now (batteries and hydrogen cells) and the overall process can be largely carbon neutral if the energy needed to make the electricity and hydrogen is itself generated sustainably
- because electric motors are quieter and less intrusive than those powered by hydrogen, the former are better suited to an urban environment, where battery recharging points can be easily provided. However, hydrogen powered units will be needed for longer distance journeys since the amount of energy stored in present-day batteries is inherently limited, thus restricting the range of electric cars and vans
- convert filling stations from supplying petrol and diesel to hydrogen and build a network of recharging points for electric cars in urban areas
- make the process of switching to a new generation of vehicles sustainable by recycling the steel from existing cars. (Ensure in the process that the energy for the recycling operation, e.g. for melting the steel, is generated from green power sources.) Stepping up the use of efficiency-improving lightweight but strong composite materials
- invest more in research and development to improve hydrogen cell and battery technology and develop recyclable new materials
- retrain workers, retool and re-equip some car assembly and component plants to make buses, trams and light rail vehicles
- retool and re-equip some component plants to make parts for an expanding green energy industry, e.g. advanced materials for windmill blades, bearings for turbines, control systems etc

To implement this programme will not require any scientific breakthroughs, all the technology needed exists now, including hydrogen cells. These cells not only have the capability to power vehicles, but in theory aircraft as well, which could solve the particular environmental problems linked to air travel. Hydrogen power is not new, but the oil companies and their political representatives have tried to stifle its introduction for the obvious reason to preserve their dominant position in the energy market. Cars using hydrogen cells are now available, but the prohibitive price means they are not widely used. The potential of hydrogen energy is heavily downplayed by environmental pressure groups, because most of them are deeply opposed to personal powered transportation. It is true that a massive expansion of public transport must be a central component of a programme to cut greenhouse gases, but if it is accepted that cars will have a useful role in a future society, albeit on a smaller scale, then the present industry will have to be made carbon neutral.

If the total number of vehicles on the road has to be significantly reduced, then in the long term there will be fewer workers in the industry and some car workers will have to be retrained to produce buses. Other workers, mainly from component factories, will have to be redeployed to different sectors, to use their skills to make parts for trains, trams and green energy machines, such as wind turbines. (This switch over will be made easier by modern robotised and computerised methods of manufacturing and design, where for example, machine tools and robots can be reprogrammed relatively easily and quickly to turn out new products.) In the short and medium term, the replacement of a proportion of existing petrol and diesel powered vehicles by electric and hydrogen fuelled cars will require all the resources of the industry. This will mean that more jobs will be needed for the conversion process involving redesign, reprogramming, retooling, retraining and manufacture.

For conversion to be carbon neutral however, it will not be sufficient just to turn out cars powered by electric motors or hydrogen cells. The electricity to charge the batteries that run the electric motors must itself be generated sustainably, which means that the energy industries must simultaneously be converted to using green energy (wind, wave and solar). More generally, the energy required to operate the production lines for the new green cars and to recycle the steel to make them, must also be green. Similarly, although burning hydrogen does not create any greenhouse gases, it does not occur naturally and so has to be manufactured, requiring an energy input that also needs to be sustainable.

Air travel accounts for a relatively small but rapidly increasing portion of greenhouse gas emissions. Because the gases are released at high altitude they cause disproportional damage to the environment. To tackle this problem, there will have to be moves away from flying to train travel, requiring the construction of a network to replace short and medium distance air journeys. This could happen very rapidly as the

Electric cars can make a contribution to cutting emissions if the energy used to power them is itself produced sustainably

experience of the London to Paris line showed, where the train very quickly won 80% of the market from the airlines. This figure could have been even higher if only a small subsidy had been introduced at the same time. To be really environmentally effective though, all the trains will have to be powered from renewable energy sources, which is not the case now.

Another area that accounts for a huge output of greenhouse gases is agriculture, including fertiliser production, usually made by burning very large quantities of fossil fuels. High fertiliser use is associated with intensive cultivation methods, which has led to soil degradation and desertification in many regions of the world. Ending such methods, which threaten millions with hunger, will deliver a big environmental dividend. Rearing cattle also makes one of the biggest contributions to global warming through methane production.

The technology to generate renewable energy is already viable and available, what is necessary is to implement it on a large scale. Reducing greenhouse gases does not therefore depend fundamentally on new research. Further research and development is needed, however, on materials to substitute for oil-based products, such as plastics. For example, high-tech reinforced ceramics could take over many of the functions of plastics, but the technology has not reached the take-off point where economies of scale will kick in and stimulate further advances. Renewable energy would be given a big boost by discovering ways of transmitting large quantities of energy over long distances. In particular, this would promote the use of solar power. The safe storage of carbon dioxide needs more research. This is important, because if coal driven power

Fertilisers used for intensive cultivation consume large amounts of fossil fuels

stations are converted to capture released carbon dioxide, the gas will have to be stored for very long periods of time underground, posing a safety hazard.

The dangers of releasing large quantities of CO_2 into the atmosphere were shown in an accident in central Africa, in which a cloud of carbon dioxide was released from a lake due to natural causes. Because it is heavier than air, the gas rolled over the countryside asphyxiating thousands of people. Until the serious hazards associated with clean coal are resolved, it will be too dangerous to implement the technology.

4.2 A socialist programme for the environment

The key elements of a programme to make society largely carbon neutral have been outlined above, but how can they be implemented? The measures required are relatively straightforward, such as switching over to renewables and developing public transport. Chapter 3 showed that current efforts by governments to address global warming are ineffective and there is little prospect of that changing. A key reason highlighted for this failure was that the ruling class has almost exclusively relied on market methods to tackle climate change.

The failure of market approaches to tackle climate change, and the problems linked to the green Keynesian alternative, point to the need for a radical policy that addresses the root of the problem: the capitalist market system and the imperialist rivalry between nation states that it has spawned in the last hundred years. Overall, a change in the social system is the only way that will allow us to live in harmony with the natural environment into the distant future. The premise for this must be the common ownership of the means of life. This will remove the causes of the inter-imperialist rivalry that is currently destroying the planet, if it is applied internationally.

In practical terms, introducing common ownership means nationalising the key industries that dominate the economy. This will need to be done throughout the world, encompassing, ultimately, the 147 multinational corporations that control 40% of global wealth and dominate the world economy. Eschewing the market system in this way, which is essential to tackle global warming, will require an alternative approach to organising production since we have seen that the operation of competitive markets degrades the environment. It will be argued here and in the next chapter, that rational democratic planning is not just a viable alternative, it also has enormous inherent advantages over the market from the point of view of saving energy. For example, it could avoid the duplication of resources , planned obsolescence and wide-scale destruction and then rebuilding of factories, plant and machinery in capitalism's slump/boom cycle.

Nationalising or renationalising the energy and transport industries will, by removing the shackles of the market, lay the basis for a switch to renewables and for the massive expansion of public transport. The industrial sectors to be included are the energy generating and distribution companies, vehicle manufacturers and bus and rail service providers. Another key aspect of the struggle to achieve a carbon neutral environment will be to increase the energy efficiency of the production of all manufactured goods and of housing. The need to reduce the intensity of energy use encompasses nearly all areas of the production of goods and services, so it will be essential to efficiently integrate the different sectors of the economy into an environmental plan. This in turn will require the public ownership of the 150 big corporations that presently dominate British society, since planning has proved to be impossible in the context of the profit-driven anarchy of capitalism.

Since it poses the greatest threat to the planet, the main focus has been on climate change and ways to mitigate its effects, but other dangers to the environment have also been highlighted. These include dangers linked to nuclear power generation in particular, but they also encompass non-nuclear toxic contamination, deforestation, unsustainable agricultural and fishing practices and species depletion. The book has attempted to show that a common factor is driving all these threats, which is the quest for profit by big corporations. At a more fundamental level, the inevitable tendency of competitive markets is to degrade the environment. For these reasons, the remedy of a democratic, planned socialist society, put forward to combat the danger of climate change, equally applies when addressing other environmental threats.

4.2.1 Are there implications for living standards and jobs?

While recognising the problem caused by global warming, many workers are nevertheless worried that the cost of converting to renewables will hit living standards and could cost them their job. It has been argued here that the ruling class will resist taking meaningful action on global warming because it is not in their short term interests. However, if they came under extreme pressure to act they would clearly attempt to do this in a capitalist context. In these circumstances, it is undoubtedly true that the resulting dislocation would cost jobs. The carbon taxes used to implement the change would also hit the living standards of the poor. However, if conversion took place in a planned manner over a period of three or four decades, where all decisions were democratically determined, and profit was not the deciding factor, then jobs and living standards would actually benefit, as will be shown. Redeployment and retraining would, of course, be necessary to achieve this outcome, but this would be done with no loss of pay.

The Stern report into the economics of tackling climate change calculated that the cost of switching over to renewables will be 1% of economic output per year over a period of approximately 40 years.[2] In Britain this corresponds to about £17bn per year, a big sum, although not compared to the amount spent on propping up the financial system after the crisis of 2008. However, as discussed in Chapter 2, it is likely that the cost could be significantly greater than £17bn per year, if global temperatures rise more sharply than Stern anticipated. When compared though to the extra resources that will be released in a socialist society with democratically run public ownership, even a tripling of the 1% per year figure would be entirely manageable, while still enhancing jobs and living standards. This can be seen by analysing five areas where the economic advantages of a socialist economy will produce savings so large that only a small proportion will be needed to pay for an environmental programme:

a) **Unemployment**. We now have again what Marx called 'a permanent army of unemployed' in the advanced capitalist countries. Even at the height of a boom companies never work at full capacity. For example, research by the House of Commons Library in 2007 found that the true cost of UK unemployment, including lost tax etc., was £28.5bn per year, at a time when the official unemployment rate was 1.7 million. (This figure excludes the cost of incapacity benefit, so is conservative.)[3] In 2011, as the recession began to bite, unemployment passed 2.5m, so the true cost by that time had risen significantly from £28.5bn. In contrast, a planned economy will be able to guarantee work for everyone with decent pay and conditions. Retraining will be provided to make sure the new jobs are meeting the needs of people, to be determined democratically.

b) **Luxury expenditure**. This will be ended for the rich. Workers in the luxury goods industries (e.g. making Rolls-Royces, luxury yachts etc.) re-deployed to fulfil more general needs. The capitalist experts are always keen to point out that ending the wealth of the rich will not solve the problems of society, because however obscenely well-off they are, there are not enough of them to make a big difference. This may be true, but nevertheless the super-rich do consume at least 5% of national income. This amounts to £85bn a year in Britain, a not inconsiderable sum that would begin the process of transforming the welfare state, as well as fixing the environment.

c) **Arms spending**. This could be massively reduced and eventually eliminated on a world scale, where the waste of resources on arms is vast, reaching nearly $1,531 trillion p.a. in 2009.[4] This sum represents approximately $1000 per year for every family on the planet, an amount of money enabling a big first step to be taken in lifting the majority of the world's population out of grinding poverty. In the UK, arms spending was $58bn in 2009 according to the Stockholm International Peace Research Institute (SIPRI). Although re-deploying hundreds of thousands of highly skilled arms workers will be a formidable task even for a planned economy, what is certain is that under capitalism such a transformation will never take place. This is because the reason for arms expenditure will not disappear, i.e. the hostility between rival capitalist countries.

d) **Eliminating the waste of capitalism**. The world is dominated by handfuls of multinational corporations who duplicate expenditure in research and development, spend unnecessary vast sums on advertising and design products with planned obsolescence. For example, rival drug companies spend billions on

Planning for the Planet: How Socialism Could Save the Enviroment

Arms spending reached $1.53trn in 2009

    developing pain killers with marginally different effectiveness and unnecessary additives for food. All of this activity is a colossal waste of resources but perfectly logical when profit is the motivating factor.

e) **Freeing the creative power of the working class.** Workers in the market system have no incentive to use much of their energy to help out the bosses. In a socialist society, on the other hand, it will be possible to release the creative instincts of employees because no fundamental conflict of interests will exist. Although a factor which is difficult to quantify, in the long run this will be the most significant advantage of socialism. It is often said by management theorists that the real experts in any firm when a problem needs to be solved are the workers themselves.

It is clear from this analysis that finding the resources for conversion to renewable energy and expanding public transport will be entirely possible in a socialist society without damaging living standards. This leaves the question of jobs, where whole new industries will have to be built and others expanded, while some contract or disappear entirely. Although highly unlikely for reasons explained in Chapter 3, if this transformation was attempted under the laws of the capitalist market, there would inevitably be huge dislocation and unemployment. Profit would be the main consideration, not the lives of the workers affected. The opposite will be the case in a socialist society, which will be able to use the techniques of democratic planning. Planning will ensure that the necessary retraining and redeployment is carried out without loss of pay or poorer working conditions. (See next chapter for details.)

To build a carbon neutral society there will be a need for more jobs, as a recent very useful and detailed study by the Campaign Against Climate Change found.[5] The report breaks down the figures for the jobs created into several categories. It calculates that if 250,000 workers were employed developing wind energy for 10 years, this renewable source could then produce three quarters of the current UK energy supply.

The renewables jobs in electricity generation will be mainly in factories making wind turbines, solar cells and marine turbines. Other new jobs in the sector will include:

- transport and assembly of turbines on site
- maintenance of wind farms and marine turbines
- transport and assembly of offshore wind and marine turbines, using the skills learned by workers in the North Sea oil and gas fields
- making barges and boats for assembling and maintaining offshore wind and marine turbines
- research and development in wave and tidal turbines
- research and development in clean coal
- training and education in the necessary skills

Many more jobs will be created in the drive to make energy use more efficient. Eighty per cent of carbon dioxide emissions originate in homes, public buildings and transport, so energy-saving will be an important complement to the switch to renewables. In this context, it could be argued that as long as it is produced from renewable sources, saving energy is not the priority. Apart from the general desirability of utilising resources efficiently, time is a factor here however, since emissions need to be reduced as quickly as possible. Speed can best be achieved by attacking the problem from both ends simultaneously.

Emissions from heating air and water could be cut by 40 - 50% over 10 years by a team of 200,000 workers, the report estimates. In addition, 100,000 workers will be needed over 10 years to renovate, insulate or replace energy inefficient public buildings. Other new jobs will be in the development and manufacture of more energy efficient domestic appliances.

Transport is a key sector that will need to be transformed (see box above on the car industry). Replacing domestic and most European air travel with rail will require large numbers of skilled jobs. The Campaign against Climate Change report calculates that if three times as many passengers used public transport, and three times as much freight went by train, figures consistent with reducing emissions by the necessary amounts, it could create 600,000 more jobs in this sector. The actual figure may not be this big, because economies of scale would kick in, but still a huge number of jobs would be generated.

The final area considered by the report is education and training. A massive programme of retraining and reskilling will be necessary, entailing large numbers of new jobs. Some of this will be on-the-job training, the remainder in colleges and universities.

Nuclear power is not covered in the CCC report, but needs urgent consideration, particularly following the disaster in Japan in 2011. Even here though, there will be no net loss of jobs when nuclear power is phased out as quickly as possible, as it needs to be. The task of decommissioning and cleaning up the atomic power stations will take many decades and will require more jobs than presently exist in the nuclear industry. For example, the ageing Dounreay plant in the North of Scotland was closed several years ago, but now employs more workers on decommissioning than it employed producing electricity.

Overall, the report works out that over 1 million net new jobs will be created, after allowing for job losses in some areas such as air transport and fossil fuel energy generation. There will also be a large number of knock-on jobs created. Jobs will be generated in manufacturers in the supply chain, for example the steel for the turbines and ships, the hammers and saws for the building workers, the paint for the buses. So, for 1 million new jobs, there will be another half a million indirect jobs.

Also, the million and a half new workers will spend more money, certainly more than they would on the dole. They will buy all sorts of consumer goods and more people will then have jobs supplying these things. The workers at those new jobs will have money to spend too, and that will create more jobs. Overall, the report estimates that after 10 years there will be a net gain of 1.6 million jobs.

Without necessarily endorsing all the detail of the Campaign against Climate Change programme for jobs, it is clear that there will be the possibility to create a substantial net increase of employment in the move to a carbon neutral society.

These job figures are for the UK, but there is a broadly similar picture for other industrialised capitalist countries with comparable economic structures, that account for the majority of emissions globally. Global warming is no respecter of national boundaries, so a programme to tackle climate change must be international. The detail will vary in different countries but the essence everywhere must be the same. Democratic public ownership will, by removing the antagonisms between nation states built into the capitalist system, enable the agreement and cooperation needed to reverse global warming.

4.2.2 Summary of a socialist environmental programme.

- Rapid conversion to the use of renewable energy sources such as wind, wave and solar power
- Big expansion of public transport
- Development of the rail network so that short and medium haul air travel can be reduced and then replaced
- Conversion of car industry to using renewable energy sources
- Research into renewable energy, such as clean coal technology and using materials not based on oil products
- Phase out nuclear power rapidly
- End unsustainable agricultural and fishing practices
- Convert the arms industry to socially useful production, including for the environment. Stop the production of energy intensive luxury goods (private jets etc.). Convert these sectors to green production
- Subsidies not carbon taxes to encourage a switch to public transport
- A programme of green jobs to tackle unemployment
- Nationalise the energy generating and transport industries
- An integrated environmental plan of production, as part of an overall plan, based on democratic public ownership of the key sectors of the economy

---

1   UK Office of National Statistics, 2002
2   *The Economics of Climate Change. The Stern Review*, by Nicolas Stern, Cambridge University Press, 2007.
3   http://www.thisislondon.co.uk/news/article-23380239-the-real-cost-of-unemployment-is-61-billion-per-year.do
4   Stockholm International Peace Research Institute, SIPRI, 2009 report.
5   One Million Climate Jobs Now, Campaign Against Climate Change, 2009, go to website for this and subsequent detailed calculations: www.climatejobs.org.

Planning for the Planet: How Socialism Could Save the Enviroment

Chapter 5:
Planned Economy and the Environment

To reiterate, the capitalist market system is destroying the environment. This is caused by the antagonism between nation states that prevents agreement on global warming, and more fundamentally, by the inexorable tendency of competitive markets to degrade the environment. To address these problems requires, first of all, taking into public ownership the big corporations that dominate the world economy, to break the destructive power of the market. This then poses the requirement for an alternative way to organise the economy, that, unlike capitalism, will allocate resources to meet human needs. The most profound of these is to ensure the survival of life on the planet in the long term. As the only alternative to the market, it will be argued here that a system of planning can efficiently allocate resources to meet need, as well as conferring other big environmental advantages, but only if it is organised democratically.

5.1 Introduction

Although Marx did not deal in any detail with how a socialist society will function, he did comment on the broad issues involved, particularly in *Critique of the Gotha Programme*. In dealing with this question, Marx was careful to warn, in his words, against writing recipes for the kitchens of the future. This warning was partly a reference to the 19th Century 'utopian socialists' who painted rosy and simplistic pictures of the socialist promised land, to lull the masses to sleep. Also, it was a recognition that socialist revolution has its own dynamic logic, as historical forces are unleashed, which confronts and solves its problems in ways that are difficult to predict.

Today, the context is significantly different in some important respects. For example, labour leaders and utopians lulling the masses to sleep with their cosy socialist visions have largely disappeared, at least for the moment. The second point Marx made regarding revolutions solving their own problems is still of course true.

Planning for the Planet: How Socialism Could Save the Enviroment

Historical circumstances have changed though in a way that requires the workings of a planned economy to be addressed in some detail. In doing this it is not the intention to try to write a blueprint for the socialist future, rather it is to indicate what the possibilities are, in reply to the legions of critics who deny even the possibility of a viable socialist planned economy.

The reasons why the mechanics of a planned economy need to be made explicit is connected partly to the collapse of the Soviet Union in 1991. This led to an ideological counter-offensive against the Left, which unfortunately succeeded in pushing back socialist consciousness a long way (the lessons of the Soviet collapse will be taken up in Chapter 6). The reason why most trade union leaders and the leaders of the former workers' parties have stopped sermonising about the socialist promised land is not because they have taken Marx's words to heart. It is because most have stopped believing in socialism in any form at all, utopian or otherwise. In this sense, the movement has been thrown back to before mass workers' parties and unions were formed in Europe in the second half of the 19th Century. These organisations were at least formally based on socialist ideas and led by people who had a commitment, in some form, to socialism.

In today's historically unprecedented circumstances, it is necessary to ideologically rearm the movement from a very basic level, a task that must include the fundamental issue of making clear how a socialist economy could function. This task has a particular urgency in relation to the environment. As has been argued here, any effective programme to tackle climate change must eschew the capitalist market system and therefore be based on a system of planning. To build support for this approach means first explaining the viability of democratic socialist planning as an alternative to capitalism and secondly how planning techniques can be deployed to resolve environmental problems.

To return to Marx. He drew on the experience of the development of capitalism and extrapolated lessons from that to give a guide, in broad terms, to the operation of socialism. In a general sense, he noted how the increasing division of labour had a tendency to socialise production, both on the shop floor and in society as a whole. This could then be manifested in the increased role of the state in production through nationalisations, which involved planning. These developments embodied elements, in an embryonic form, of the organisation of a future socialist society. Marx also referred to worker co-ops in a similar way, describing them as a new mode of production 'within the old form' (*Capital*, Vol. 3, Chapter 27). The same could be said now of the planning of production to the exclusion of the market within large corporations. Beyond these general extrapolations from capitalism, Marx confined himself to some brief comments on the socialist mode of production as that of 'self-government of the producers'.

After Marx, Karl Kautsky, an early follower and populariser of Marx, although later to move to the right, made a significant point in 1902 emphasising the importance of democratic structures and organisation in a planned economy.[1] The 'Austro-Marxist', Otto Neurath, in the 1920s made some comments on planning the use of natural resources and anticipated to some extent current debates on the 'limits to growth'.[2] Following these relatively isolated interventions, from the 1920s onwards, debates on planning were not surprisingly dominated by what was happening in Russia, where a socialist state had been proclaimed after the revolution of 1917. The controversies surrounding this event, including the so-called socialist calculation debate, will be taken up in Chapter 6. Before that some detail needs to be given about how planning can function in general terms, before considering the particular problems associated with the Soviet Union.

5.2 The elements of Planned Economy

Planning is allocating resources of labour and materials for the production of goods and services for the benefit of society as a whole, rather than to make profits for the capitalists. An important point to reiterate is that planning is not primarily a technical question. Rather, its success will depend on creating organs through which the working class can democratically control production from the workplace upwards. The key element will be the conscious control of working people, on a day to day basis, of the decisions that shape their lives.

Planning will operate at three levels, nationally and internationally, at industry or sectoral level and at the individual enterprise. Considering these in turn:

a) The overall performance of the economy will be decided at the national and international level. There will be targets for productivity growth, investment, consumption and of course sustainability, which will be determined democratically by institutions created after the removal of capitalism. Here the decisions about the priorities that society must have in the initial stages, for example, between health expenditure, housing or the environment, will be made.

b) At the sectoral level, it will be necessary to determine consumer demand for the goods or services of that particular industry. The efficient exchange of materials and semi-finished products with other sectors, e.g. from suppliers must be organised. Demand is determined by obtaining information from powerful proactive consumer bodies and by using the very sophisticated tools for market research developed under capitalism. To organise the movement of goods between industries, avoiding bottlenecks, it will be possible to use techniques such as operational research, developed by the big capitalist monopolies to plan the complex movement of goods between their operations around the world.

c) Planning at the enterprise level. The methods mentioned in b) above, i.e. consumer committees and market research, will also be used to determine consumer needs and preferences. It is also likely that as far as enterprises making some consumer products are concerned (as opposed to capital goods manufacturers), some market mechanisms will be retained in the transition from capitalism. This could involve small businesses or worker co-ops, but only within the framework of a nationalised economy. If the market sector was too large it would threaten to impose its inherent inequalities onto society.

Since Marx's day, and particularly after the Russian Revolution, academics have written libraries full of books about why socialism cannot work. To get a flavour of the polemic, this is what Ludwig Von Mises, one of the most prominent academic critics of socialist planning, wrote in the 1920s:

'...a socialist order of society is unrealisable. All efforts to realise Socialism lead only to the destruction of society. Factories, mines and railways will come to a standstill, towns will be deserted. The population of the industrial territories will die out or migrate elsewhere. .... Nomad tribes from the Eastern steppes would again raid and pillage Europe, sweeping across it with swift cavalry. Who could resist them in the thinly populated land left defenceless after the weapons inherited from the higher technique of capitalism had worn out?'[3]

His and other criticisms on the 'impossibility' of socialism will be taken up in more detail in Chapter 6. It is only necessary here to briefly respond to some key points. One of the main arguments is that planning the efficient allocation of resources is impossible because of the vast complexity of modern industrial society where millions of economic transactions take place every day. However, many of these economic interactions are between enterprises, they do not involve consumers. It is quite clear that present day multinational firms conduct planning of a similar complexity to that required under socialism all the time. The activity of the multinationals answers a further criticism that the operation of supply and demand to determine price is the only efficient way to proceed in the exchange of goods. In their international operations, companies like General Motors simply allocate resources between countries and factories.

As far as planning for consumer needs is concerned, the key point is that active democratic institutions should exist that can compel the planning bodies to respond to their demands. Techniques such as market research and using the internet will make the tasks faced by future socialist planners enormously easier than those tasks their counterparts had to deal with in the young Soviet Union. It is important not to exaggerate the role that will be played by the internet or look for a 'technical fix'- the existence of democratic institutions will be paramount. The role of democratically elected and powerful consumer bodies will make sure that shoddy goods are not

In their international operations big corporations simply allocate resources between countries and factories

produced and quality is maintained. Advances in modern production management techniques can be applied. It is probable that the future socialist society will inherit, unlike the Soviet Union, an industrial tradition, or culture, associated with the highest levels of technique developed by capitalism. It is very unlikely that the devastating conditions that accompanied the birth of the Soviet Union, a huge shackle on its development, will be repeated. This issue will be developed in Chapter 6.

Democratic, rational planning will permit a consistent improvement in ecological conditions to be achieved over many decades until full sustainability is reached. Above all, the condition of the environment will not be subject to the whim of the capitalist market, where it will always have a low priority. Of the three sectors of a socialist economy mentioned above, the most important for the environment is the first, that is planning at the national and particularly international level. Here it will be a question of the direct allocation of resources to fulfil improvements that have been democratically agreed in all countries. The planning bodies will organise the progressive replacement of fossil fuel energy sources with renewables and the elimination of non-recyclable materials. Investment will be directed to low environmentally-intensive sectors, such as public transport. Research aimed at promoting sustainability, that could include new non-polluting energy sources for private transportation or electricity generation, will also be important.

In the broader economy it will be necessary, when setting planned growth targets, to make sure that the costs of environmental damage are not included in the definition of 'growth', as happens under capitalism. In other words, the target for economic growth used by the planning bodies will exclude the economic activity generated by cleaning up pollution. This will be accounted for separately, so that there is no danger of a hidden incentive to pollute being built into the plan. Although attempts to differentiate pollution clean-up effects from other growth in a capitalist economy, by measuring a 'sustainability' gap,[4] have raised problems, these would be avoided in a planned system.

Other keys to ecological transformation, such as developing new technology, will be achieved by direct allocation of investment. Market mechanisms will at most play a marginal role in an overall environmental plan, although, for example, using the price system to ration the use of environmentally wasteful luxury goods could be employed.

5.3 Planning Techniques

To get a full understanding of how a planned economy will work, it is now necessary to look in more detail at the elements that constitute a planned approach to running the economy, in particular how they impact on the environment. The period immediately after the replacement of the capitalist system will be one of transition to a fully developed socialist society, which will be where all human needs have been met and environmental problems resolved. During the transition period, planning will permit the coordination of economic activities so that these dual aims can progressively be achieved, although tackling both simultaneously will pose additional challenges. However, action on meeting human needs cannot be postponed, not least since this is a prerequisite to addressing global warming. It will remove the antagonisms that prevent cooperation on environmental issues. This will be explained in the next chapter.

Equally action to tackle climate change cannot be postponed either, since all the scientific evidence points to the need for urgency. To reconcile the twin aims of the plan, it is essential that the expansion of the means of production to meet human needs is done sustainably. The key measures to achieve this will be converting energy generation to renewables, switching to a more eco-friendly lifestyle, primarily by expanding public transport, and improving the general energy efficiency of all sectors of the economy. As has already been commented on, eliminating the waste inherent in capitalist society will be a big step in achieving this last aim.

Not least because meeting human need is a prerequisite for tackling climate change, environmental problems cannot be viewed in isolation from, or necessarily as having priority over, addressing the other evils of capitalism. For example, a plan for the economy must also solve issues such as the mass unemployment that is endemic under capitalism in virtually all countries of the world. Away from the profit driven anarchy of the market system, this goal can be easily built into a plan of production. Take a simple example for illustrative purposes. If the policy goal is to remove unemployment in five years then the growth in output that this will require can be calculated. If current unemployment is 20%, and if the underlying planned productivity (output per worker) growth is 3% per year, and the working population is increasing by 1% per year, then growth would need to be [3+1+(20/5)] = 8%.

If at the same time, a goal is to increase consumption in society by a certain amount to fulfil other urgent social needs, this will require either increased productivity or an increased number brought into employment over the period. Whether these increases in turn can be delivered will depend on the possibilities for technological change based on the increased investment in the plan. It will also depend on whether the existing capital stock (machinery etc.) permits a proportionate increase in production as the labour force is expanded. These are concrete questions that can only be decided at the time. However, the issue will be posed of making choices between desirable social outcomes, for instance, a trade off between the time taken to eliminate unemployment and increasing consumption. These choices will be taken democratically, in full view and with the participation of everyone involved, in contrast to the crucial decisions that affect lives under capitalism, that are hidden from society.[5]

As with other social questions, environmental issues cannot be excluded from the need to make choices between competing priorities in a transitional epoch. As has already been explained, action cannot be postponed in any significant way on tackling climate change. There will be limited room for manoeuvre in accommodating competing demands. Since the Stern report[6] calculated that it would take only 1% of economic output per year, albeit over several decades, to tackle climate change, how quickly other social priorities can be implemented when environmental aims are included in the plan, should not be greatly affected. Even if the 1% figure is an underestimate, the scale of the compromises needed will still be relatively small and will not prevent achieving other aims, such as eliminating unemployment.

Consumer Choice

Once the plan is established at national level and coordinated internationally, the detail needs to be filled in and made concrete at sectoral, sub-sectoral and ultimately down to household level. For the latter case, a crucial area will be in making sure that the plan is in harmony with the shifting patterns of consumer tastes and preferences. As awareness grows of environmental dangers, these consumer preferences will increasingly reflect changes in behaviour in an eco-friendly direction. The range of consumer choice accommodated in a planned economy is a potentially controversial area, particularly as excessive choice impacts on the environment in terms of waste and duplication. On the other hand, critics of planning claim that it will result in a grey and monolithic society devoid of consumer choice.

In fact 'choice' under capitalism is often bogus. 'Consumer choice', which has an almost mythical iconic status on the neo-liberal agenda, often does not mean real choice for most people. This is true particularly in education, health or public transport. It is also environmentally wasteful, as for example in the production of a dozen varieties of near identical toothpaste. The de-regulation of bus services is a good example of a measure ostensibly meant to increase choice. This eventually led to less bus use, causing more pollution and reduced choice, due to the re-monopolisation of the industry that took place on a private basis.

A balance is required between resource use efficiency and providing a sufficient range of commodities to satisfy, in the first place, needs, and then varying tastes. Exactly where the balance is struck must be democratically decided. In this process the consumer voice must be heard as well as that of the producers, expressed through institutions with real power, independent of the planning bodies. Another related issue, subject to much discussion by socialists in the past, is how far commodities destined for consumer consumption should be produced by non-nationalised bodies such as co-ops, mutuals or small and medium-sized private businesses. This question will be taken up briefly in the next chapter.

Deregulation of bus services eventually led to less consumer choice

Techniques to determine consumer preferences have been developed to very sophisticated levels under capitalism. As early as the 19th Century, researchers had noticed how consumer tastes and patterns of consumption changed with the development of the economy. In particular, as income increased the proportion spent on food declined. Within this category, demand for basic foodstuffs fell as incomes rose, with the popularity of 'luxury' items moving in the opposite direction. Today, consumer behaviour is monitored in real time, on-line, even to the extent of analysing each individual's spending patterns and drawing up profiles to target them for advertising. This, of course, is in the pursuit of profit and is an unacceptable invasion of privacy.

In a planned economy there will be no need to micro-analyse consumer behaviour in this way; understanding longer-term patterns will be sufficient for efficient planning. But the current consumer monitoring capability does answer those critics, such as Von Mises, quoted at the beginning of this chapter, who thought it was impossible for a plan ever to assimilate the millions of individual decisions made by consumers each day across an economy. He claimed the 'hidden hand' of the market was the only mechanism that could do this. It is important to reiterate what was also written at the beginning of this chapter, that the most important factor for the efficient operation of a planned economy will be the existence of democratic bodies of producers and consumers with real power to control the planning organs. In this sense, there is no technical fix, however advanced the technology, because having detailed accurate information on which to base a plan of production is a necessary but not sufficient condition for its efficient operation. Unless the planners and their political masters are accountable to society they will tend to act in their own interests, as experience in the Soviet Union showed, and derail the objectives of the plan.

5.3.1 Input-Output Analysis

The next stage in the planning process is to bring together the social aims of the plan. For example, the need to eliminate unemployment in a certain period of time, together with the information on consumer needs and preferences and the environmental requirements to tackle climate change. The implications of achieving the goals of the plan for the smooth running of the economy, the capacity in the various sectors and sub-sectors that must be ensured and brought into balance, etc., need to be analysed. Input-Output analysis is a very powerful tool to do this. It was created by Wassily Leontief, with work that began with his research at Petrograd University in the Soviet Union in the 1920s when studying the problems of planning (see box on Leontief).

Wassily Leontief

Leontief made a very significant contribution to the economics of planning with his development of Input-Output theory, a theoretical tool viewing an economy as a multi-dimensional system. In the model interrelationships are analysed and the needs of social policy, micro data at the household, firm and sectoral levels, and the operation of national and international economies, are brought together. It is potentially a very powerful tool for planning a socialist economy. Leontief began to develop his idea when he researched the Soviet economy at the then Petrograd (subsequently Leningrad, and now St Petersburg) University in the USSR in the early 1920s.

In 1973, he was awarded the Nobel prize for economics for Input-Output theory. Although he began his work in the Soviet Union, and was influenced by Marx's theories of the reproduction of capital, he was not a Marxist economist and spent much of his subsequent life in the mainstream of Western academic economics. He always explicitly acknowledged Marx's influence on his theory,[7,8] although the extent of his debt to Marx became a subject of controversy when Soviet economists, after ignoring I/O for decades, adopted his idea in the late 1950s.[9] He used and developed ideas that he thought useful in a heterodox manner and in this spirit was highly critical of the neo-liberal direction bourgeois economics took in his later life. As a result he became marginalised from mainstream academic thinking.

When he was awarded the Nobel prize in 1973, ideas around national accounting and planning capitalist economies were in vogue, albeit to a limited extent. These ideas seemed feasible to some in the context of the relatively stable and expansionary conditions of the post-war boom (that ended in the crises of 1973-6). After 1976, as the so-called 'golden age' receded from memory, capitalist development reverted to a more historically usual convulsive character, bringing in its train neo-liberal orthodoxy. By the 1990s, it is very doubtful that a Nobel economics prize would have been given for work that was both indebted to Marx's ideas and was associated with planning. An incidental ironic post-script to Leontief's work was also revealed after the financial crash of 2008, which was associated with staggeringly complex and impenetrable mathematical models. In academic circles, Leontief was regarded as a pioneer of mathematical economics, since he was gifted in this direction and Input-Output theory naturally lent itself to a mathematical treatment. But he would almost certainly have been highly critical of the misuse of mathematics underlying the speculation that triggered the 2008 crisis.

Wassily Leontief was born in Munich in 1905 into a middle class Russian family. He spent his childhood in St Petersburg in a milieu with radical traditions. His father was an academic who studied Marxism and researched the economic situation of Russian workers. His mother's brother was imprisoned by the Tsarist authorities for revolutionary activity[10] and subsequently executed for participating in a prisoner rebellion. Leontief entered the socio-economic department of Petrograd University in 1920 at the early age of 15. By 1925, he had published a paper that made a significant contribution to planning theory, by discovering a problem of double counting in national accounts made by the Soviet statistical bureau.[11] This work must have subsequently informed his Input-Output theory, when he returned to it 10 years later.

Leontief, after clashing with the Soviet authorities on the question of academic freedom, left the USSR in 1925 to carry out research in Germany. He then went to the USA in the 30s where he resumed his Input-Output work. In this activity, his historical references were Quesnay, the French physiocratic economist of the 18th Century, and Marx, who developed Quesnay's *Tableau Economique* for his schema for simple capital reproduction in Volume 2 of *Capital*. (The Physiocrats believed, contrary to Marx, that the ultimate source of all wealth was from the land.) Marx then used his formula for simple reproduction to address the so-called transformation problem of how to convert values into prices of production. His intention was not to use the reproduction equations in a way that could be used for planning purposes. Leontief, however, using the ideas of Marx as a starting point, developed them into a powerful tool that could analyse the interdependencies of the sectors of an economy. He realised the potential in Marx's formula for doing this and then systematised it. He also saw the possibilities of applying Input-Output theory to address environmental issues, at a time when the problems and dangers in this area were only beginning to be understood.

Leontief came to the West in the 1930s and applied his idea to firms and national economies, particularly the USA. (In the post war boom, when conditions were relatively stable, it appeared that his technique was useful in predicting economic performance.)

Input-Output analysis determines the relations between the branches of a economy, national or international. Leontief's original Input-Output table refers to eleven branches of industry plus agriculture, transport and households. It is in the form of a matrix with the branches arranged horizontally and vertically. The horizontal rows show what each of the 14 branches sells to the 13 others, while the vertical columns show what resources each branch buys from the others. As a simple starting point, assume that the relations between different branches remain stable, e.g. an increase in wind turbine production of 10% needs an increase of 10% in steel supplied by another branch of industry. Technical coefficients can in this way be worked out between all branches of production, up to virtually any number, and can be of a very complex nature, easily handled however by computers. The result is that predictions can be made about resources needed to fulfil a particular requirement of the plan.

Leontief's Input-Output (I/O) analysis was influenced by Marx's theory of capital reproduction and growth, his first 'closed' model using the same assumptions of equilibrium as simple reproduction theory. It is necessary to explain here the connections between Marx's ideas and such an important planning technique as I/O. This is important first to understand its basis, since I/O has its historical roots in Marx's theory and secondly to set the record straight, since Marx's influence on Leontief is contested. Taking up this debate is also important in the struggle to rehabilitate the concept of a socialist planned economy, particularly as it is applied to the environment (see Appendix 1). It is also worth being aware of I/O's Marxist roots when using data from official publications to analyse environmental problems. Their presentation of the statistics is based on standard accounting procedures using market prices. Prices of production derived from Marxist value categories are shown in Appendix 1.

Although Leontief intended I/O to be used in a capitalist economy, this does not mean that capitalism can be planned. The technique can give useful pointers to the workings of a market system nevertheless (see box on Planning Capitalism?).

Planning Capitalism?

The idea of planning capitalist economies had its heyday in the 1950s and 1960s during the relative stability of the post-war boom that bred reformist illusions (i.e. that it is possible to fundamentally reform capitalism). Having elements of planning along side a market system was seen as a way of controlling its excesses. That the process went quite a long way is surprising now in an epoch of neo-liberal dominance, with the Labour government of the 1960s having a five year plan for the economy when it came into power. In France, a state planning institute, the Commissariat du Plan, was established, mimicking superficially GOSPLAN, the Soviet planning body. In the Netherlands, the 'Planburo' was set up, along with examples in other countries. The policy objectives of its supporters were always very limited, to nationalise and plan a few 'key' economic sectors, as a way of keeping in check the excesses of market. This was at a time when the ruling class was looking over its shoulder at a militant working class and the Soviet Union was still seen as an alternative model to capitalism.

The approach taken of limited nationalisation was fundamentally flawed. Either the nationalised sector was so small that it had no influence on the economy as a whole, and so planning was ineffective. Alternatively, if it threatened to grow to a more dominant position, retaliation from the capitalists in terms of disinvestment - a strike of capital - would take place, therefore disrupting and undermining the aims of the plan. In Britain, when more extensive nationalisation seemed a great threat, elements of the bourgeoisie even plotted a military coup against the Labour government in the

1960s. As long as private property exists, capitalism cannot function unless the 'rules of the game' are observed, which are centred on the quest for profit. Nationalisations can be carried out inside this framework, if the intention is to nationalise losses or to bail out sick industries. The Labour government did this after the Second World War and when it took over indebted banks in 2008. Planning in these circumstances becomes meaningless in terms of planning to meet the needs of society.

In practice, planning in capitalist countries amounted to not much more than forecasting the future development of the economy, extrapolated from past experience. This approach had some success when conditions were relatively stable and expanding, but only in helping the capitalists identify the most profitable area for investment, not in solving any underlying social problems. Governments sometimes set targets for growth, but these were not compulsory on big business, they were just guidelines that could be ignored if desired. No sanction, such as setting up an alternative public enterprise, was applied when the guidelines were not met. Rather, the tactic of the state was then to offer incentives to encourage the bosses to invest in the chosen sectors. These incentives often took the form of hidden subsidies delivered through the nationalised industries, in the form of artificially low prices. The managers of the state run industries were often former senior executives from the companies that received the subsidies directly or indirectly, so understood very well what was expected of them.

The result was that nationalisation and 'planning', run on a bureaucratic and capitalist basis, became discredited in the eyes of some, if not most workers. They correctly saw it as a way of propping up the market system and rewarding idle and incompetent bosses at their expense. A section of the most class-conscious in the working class realised that there was an alternative, based on democratic planning and workers' control and management of the economy. In any event, the whole bogus facade of planning was swept away with the end of the post-war boom along with the stable conditions that helped it. It was replaced by convulsive change that no mathematical model was able to predict, as the events of 2008 demonstrated.

The fate of Leontief's Input-Output theory in many ways mirrored the changes in capitalism since WW2. As noted earlier, it won a Nobel prize in the early 70s, but then became increasingly marginalised, as he did himself, from the neo-liberal academic mainstream. This is because it is a model that works with parameters of the real economy, for instance predicting what will happen to emissions if final demand in the economy is changed by a certain amount. It is useful for planning purposes and became popular in environmental analysis partly because it could so easily combine physical units and prices. However, the model contains none of the dogma of neo-classical economics that came to dominate in the current neo-liberal phase of capitalism. For instance, profit-maximising and other behavioural assumptions of neo-

> classical economics that exclude the interests of society, play no role in it.
> There are no supply and demand equations or capacity constraints - linked to 'supply-side' factors - such as deregulating 'inflexible' labour markets, that neo-classical theory prioritises. As a consequence, in environmental analysis, the initial attraction of the model faded. The emphasis moved from real economy calculations to price theory. For example, at what level to set the price of a 'permit to pollute' in order to create a sufficient incentive to meet an emissions target. This information was needed to operationalise the permit trading system on which the Kyoto treaty was based, an endeavour incidentally that proved futile.

Before moving on to look at its application to environmental issues, for clarification, a simple explanation of an Input-Output table is given in Appendix 2. The table is developed using standard accounting conventions. Such tables, that show the potential the technique has to aid planning, are found in official publications, albeit in more complicated forms.

In a planned economy, final demand - household consumption, investment, etc. - first for the whole economy, and then sectorally, will be democratically decided according to social and environmental needs. The output from each sector and sub-sector that this political decision requires will then be worked out through Input-Output tables. Planners will then ensure that each industry is provided with enough capacity to deliver this socially determined level of consumption.

5.3.2. Planning for the environment.

Consider the standard industrial categories, shown below, used to model the UK economy.[20] The key sectors to be considered for environmental planning purposes are: electricity production, transport, manufacturing, agriculture and construction.

Agriculture, forestry & fishing	Distribution & hotels
Mining & quarrying	Transport & communication
Manufacturing	Finance & business services
Electricity, gas & water supply	Public administration & defence
Construction	Education, health & social work
	Other services

The most important point is that fossil fuel inputs to energy generation will have to be largely substituted by renewables. Coal, oil and gas use will have to be reduced by approximately 70% to achieve the minimum targets for tackling climate change. To do this will require expanding investment in wind, wave and solar power and phasing out most electricity generated from fossil fuel. Another major area that will be affected will be transport, where investment for making renewable power sources for cars and for expanding the railway and bus network will be needed.

The overall output of the Energy and Transport sectors would not necessarily change by substituting for renewables, even though car use would fall, as would air travel. Even if it turned out there was an overall contraction in output in these sectors, in Manufacturing there would be an increase due to the new investment proposed, leading to a net increase in jobs, as was seen in Chapter 4. All the parameters connected with these decisions, based on democratically decided policy, would have to be fed into an I/O model to predict exactly what the result will be to the overall economy. At this stage, this result would have to be reconciled with social needs, similarly democratically decided, that would have also been submitted to the plan in terms of consumption and employment etc.

The measures outlined above are the crucial ones needed for tackling global warming. However, in parallel there is a need to increase energy efficiency across the whole economy that can make a contribution to cutting greenhouse gases. In this task, I/O, as well as giving us a model of the whole economy, can be applied to solving specifically environmental problems. It is particularly flexible since physical quantities can easily be combined with economic data in the tables to study their interdependence. This can give useful insights to assist optimisation of energy use.

Bio-mass

Leontief realised very early, as soon as environmental issues began to gain prominence in the late 1960s, the potential of I/O methods in this area. At that time energy conservation was seen as a crucial issue. Not because of the need to cut greenhouse gases, since that problem had not yet emerged, but because it was thought there was going to be an energy shortage. To give an example of how interdependencies exist in energy production, consider the currently controversial question of bio-mass. The general observation that energy conservation measures also use up energy themselves is particularly relevant to bio-mass production, where the net benefits are highly doubtful. For instance, the agricultural products used to produce bio-mass may be transported in lorries that use petrol, and the digging of tunnels that the lorries might use on their journey requires huge amounts of energy.[21]

Realisation of this problem lead to the concept of 'net energy', in which the energy used up by a proposed activity is subtracted from what it contributes. It became clear though that this was insufficient, since it did not recognise the complexity of the process, where inputs are required to make inputs stretching down a long chain. For example, the lorries carrying the bio-mass, themselves had to be built and energy used in this process, as did the assembly line that was used to build the lorries and so on. There is clearly a complicated and extensive system of sectoral interdependencies needing to be quantified to understand if an energy saving initiative is worthwhile. I/O methods are extremely well suited to do this.

An analysis of energy use for the whole US economy employing Input-Output calculations gave some dramatic results. The normal approach of just considering directly used inputs overlooked, on average, 60% of the true quantity of the energy used. Even if a second round was considered, i.e. the inputs to make the direct inputs, 28% of energy use was still omitted. When analysing the key issue of global warming, it is important to avoid this problem and to get a true picture allowing for the interdependencies between sectors, by using I/O methods. To see concretely how such an approach can be applied to optimising energy use, look at the following example:

Referring to standard industrial categories, consider a simple two sector economy, consisting of Agriculture and Manufacturing, where we are trying to reduce the use of oil. Suppose Manufacturing uses one million tonnes of oil a year and Agriculture, let us assume, none. While Agriculture uses no oil directly, it does buy commodities from the manufacturing sector, (farm machinery, etc.) that themselves required oil for their manufacture. In other words, of the total use of oil by Manufacturing, some part of it is attributable to the production of agricultural commodities. Quantifying these factors allows us to investigate, for example, the effect on oil consumption of introducing a change in technology. If the new technology reduces by half the amount of commodities that Agriculture needs to buy from Manufacturing, oil use in the economy is reduced from 1 million tonnes to 845,000 (the theory behind this is in Appendix 2). This reduction arose from a technological change that appeared to have no direct connection to energy, but which is revealed by the I/O model. This outcome may not have been totally unexpected in this simple case, in view of Agriculture's inputs from Manufacture. In a real analysis of a multi-sector model it would, however, give useful insights into technological changes that could optimise energy use, which could not easily be predicted.

Analysing global warming using I/O methods

Another example of the insights provided by I/O methods is taken from an analysis of the Australian economy in the crucial area of carbon dioxide emissions.[22] An accurate estimate of the quantity of carbon dioxide emitted by every sector can be calculated. It is useful in this process to work out the intensity of carbon dioxide output, defined as the total emissions in a sector divided by the final demand. In other words, how much pollution occurs per unit of final demand, e.g. per million $A in this example. The table below shows the economy divided into standard industrial categories in the left column. Carbon dioxide intensities are in the next column and the quantity or level of carbon dioxide in tonnes in the third. The right hand column shows the level as a percentage of the total level. The figures in brackets are rankings.

Take the first sector as an example, 'Agriculture, forestry fishing'. This gives a high figure, both for level and intensity which is at first sight counter-intuitive, since it exceeds several polluting manufacturing sectors. The high number is a result of the large amount of fertiliser used in agriculture, which requires significant amounts of fossil fuel for processing, an interdependence revealed by the model. (The surprisingly low percentage that electricity appears to contribute to the carbon dioxide level, at 14.99% of the total, is surprising, since power stations contribute far more to emissions. The answer is that the majority of output of power stations goes to other sectors before it is emitted, only a relatively small amount goes direct to consumers, the figure shown here.)

The table shows the sectors high in intensity of carbon use which need to be prioritised when considering ways to mitigate emissions, thus giving a guide to planners. As has already been discussed, the priority for any plan must be sharply reducing the fossil fuel used in energy generation, which will cut CO_2 intensities and level. Beyond that the table is very useful in highlighting the areas where further energy efficiencies can be most easily obtained. For example, the high carbon intensity rankings of most manufacturing sectors indicates that research could be done on new technology to improve efficiencies in these areas.

The table also shows absolute levels of emissions, where service sectors are very high in the rankings. This does not mean that seeking energy efficiency gains in these areas should be prioritised, since the high ranking is due to the very large relative size of these industries compared to manufacturing. The intensity of energy use in services is, as the table shows, very low in ranking order, showing to a planner that the scope for applying new technology or more energy efficient working practices to gain improvements is limited. A sharp reduction in fossil fuel use will probably cut emissions sufficiently in these sectors, without looking for further major gains.

This chapter has tried to show the potential that democratic planning has to replace the market system as a way of efficiently allocating resources, as well as the particular advantages for tackling environmental problems that planning provides. The view cited at the beginning of the chapter by the academic critic Von Mises, that a modern society organised on socialist lines is impossible, has begun to be answered in concrete terms as far as one aspect of socialism is concerned, that of planning. However, the claimed technical impossibility of planning due to the complexity of industrial society is just one aspect of the barrage of anti-socialist propaganda emerging since the collapse of the Soviet Union. The next chapter will take on these other attacks, some of the most serious of which relate directly to environmental questions.

Carbon Dioxide intensity and level			
Sector	CO2 intensity[a]	CO2 level[b]	% of total level
Agriculture, forestry, fishing	1.80 (6)	13.83 (8)	4.71
Mining	0.98 (11)	9.95 (12)	3.41
Meat and milk products	1.03 (10)	8.51 (13)	2.92
Food products	1.53 (8)	11.54 (10)	4
Beverages and tobacco	0.92 (12)	3.39 (20)	1.17
Textiles, clothing and footwear	0.55 (24)	3.06 (21)	1.05
Wood, wood products, furniture	0.88 (14)	2.03 (23)	0.7
Paper products, printing, publishing	0.87 (15)	1.39 (24)	0.48
Chemicals	1.23 (9)	2.57 (22)	0.88
Petrol and coal products	10.72 (2)	37.78 (2)	12.95
Non-metallic mineral products	2.19 (5)	0.35 (26)	0.12
Basic metal products	4.49 (4)	20.25 (4)	6.94
Fabricated metal products	1.70 (7)	3.48 (19)	1.19
Transport equipment	0.74 (20)	4.70 (17)	1.61
Machinery and equipment	0.88 (13)	5.29 (16)	1.82
Miscellaneous manufacturing	0.77 (18)	1.01 (25)	0.35
Electricity	15.24 (1)	43.74 (1)	14.99
Gas	9.96 (3)	4.67 (18)	1.6
Water	0.66 (22)	0.20 (27)	0.07
Construction	0.75 (19)	28.11 (3)	9.64
Wholesale and retail, repairs	0.49 (25)	18.22 (5)	6.25
Transport, storage, communication	0.81 (17)	13.38 (9)	4.58
Finance, property, business services	0.62 (23)	5.71 (14)	1.96
Residential property	0.19 (27)	5.50 (15)	1.89
Public administration	0.84 (16)	14.35 (7)	4.92
Community services	0.44 (26)	17.80 (6)	6.1
Recreational services	0.72 (21)	10.83 (11)	3.71
Total	–	291.75	100

a-tonnes x 10^3/$A x 10^6 b-tonnes x 10^6
Sectoral distribution of carbon dioxide emissions.

Appendix 1

The influence on Input-Output methods of Marx's theory of capital reproduction.

The central premise of Input-Output (I/O) analysis, that each sector of the economy must sell to the other sectors the same as it buys from them, is a development and enlargement of the conditions of equilibrium. Marx derived these initially for the simple reproduction of capital, then extended them to expanded reproduction. Marx divided an economy into two sectors, those producing capital and consumer goods, (Departments I and II, using the terminology in Capital).

For an economy to be in equilibrium, i.e. not encountering overproduction for example, Marx postulated that supply and demand must balance for the two categories of commodities from Depts. I and II. Let us assume that the supply to the capital goods sector (e.g. the machinery for making consumer goods) is $Ic + Iv + Is$ and that to consumer goods is $IIc + IIv + IIs$. Here, c is constant capital (e.g. raw materials and machinery), v, variable capital (wages) and s, surplus value (profit). Then, after analysing what constituted the demand for these commodities, Marx calculated that for equilibrium under conditions of simple reproduction:

$$IIc = Iv + Is$$

(The assumptions for simple reproduction are that all the constant capital, (raw materials, machinery etc.) is consumed or worn out and has to be replaced each year, and that all surplus value (profit) is likewise consumed, i.e. no capital is accumulated and nothing is reinvested.)

For the derivation of the equilibrium formula, see a text on Marxist economics.[12] What it is saying is that $Iv + Is$, i.e. the wages paid and profit in the capital goods sector, which is the total demand for consumer goods created by the production of capital goods, equals IIc, i.e. the constant capital to be replaced in the consumer goods sector. This represents the total demand for capital goods created by the production of consumer goods. It is clear that there must be an interaction between the two sectors, since, for example, workers in Dept. I will stimulate demand in Dept. II, by spending some of their wages on consumer goods.

Put another way, what the equation is saying is that the economy is in equilibrium when the production of capital goods gives rise to a demand for consumer goods equal to the demand for capital goods to which the production of consumer goods gives rise. Or in other words, the market is in balance when reciprocal supply and demand is equal between the two sectors.[13] If Marx's equilibrium condition is now compared to that used by Leontief in his I/O analysis of the US economy done in the thirties, they can be shown to be the same,[14,15] which gives significant weight to the case for Marx being his most important influence. Another clue to the influence of Marx on I/O is found in his Grundrisse.[16] Here he develops Quesnay's *Tableau Économique* into this multi-sector model of interdependencies in an idealised economy:

	For Labour	Raw material	Machinery	Surplus product	Total
A Raw material manufacturer	20	40	20	20	100
B Ditto	20	40	20	20	100
C Machinery manufacturer	20	40	20	20	100
D Worker's necessaries	20	40	20	20	100
E Surplus producer	20	40	20	20	100

Here the figures in the table, which is in matrix form, anticipating Leontief's use of mathematics in economics, are given as percentages. The percentages represent fixed coefficients defining the flows between the sectors. Marx used the table to analyse for example, the effect on output proportions if the surplus product is spent on increased production rather than on luxury items (E in the table). These points reveal a very similar approach to the later work of Leontief, further reinforcing the case of Marx's influence on I/O.

Marx's 'Tableau' has been adapted further, that makes the similarity with I/O clearer.[17] Here the conditions of equilibrium for the expanded reproduction of capital are applied to a four sector economy where capital goods are divided into two sectors. These are fixed capital (A) and raw materials and power (B), (both Dept I). Consumer goods are divided into current goods(C) and luxury goods (D) (both Dept. II).

If the output of the economy is expressed as, for example, :

1000c + 500v + 500s = 2000 A
3000c + 1500v + 1500s = 6000 B
2000c + 1000v + 1000s = 4000 C
400c + 200v + 200s = 800 D

it can be shown that applying the equilibrium condition for expanded reproduction gives the following table, which reveals the mutual interactions of the economy between sectors, where the horizontal rows show what is sold by one sector to another and the vertical columns what is bought:

Planned Economy and the Environment

	A	B	C	D	Total	
A	312.5	937.5	625	125	2000	8000 I
B	937.5	2812.5	1875	375	6000	
C	625	1875	1250	250	4000	4800 II
D	125	375	250	50	800	
Total	2000	6000	4000	800	12800	
		8000 I		4800 II		

In so far as it shows a balance of what is sold by one sector to another, shown in the rows, and what is bought, shown in the columns, the structure of this table resembles a standard I/O table. The comparison cannot be carried too far though, since the table above was constructed from Marxist value categories rather than market prices on which standard I/O tables are based, and so differs in very significant ways.

Appendix 2
A simple example demonstrating Input-Output methods using standard accounting conventions.

For the purpose of demonstration, consider how an I/O transaction table is constructed that consists of just two industrial sectors, Agriculture and Manufacturing.[19] Although in a simplified form, the following table is consistent with what is found in transaction tables in official statistics:

Input-Output Transaction Table

All figures $ million	Sales to:			
Purchases from:	Agriculture	Manufacturing	Final Demand	Total Output
Agriculture	0	200	800	1000
Manufacturing	600	0	1400	2000
Primary Inputs				
Wages	300	1200		
Other factor payments	100	600		
Total Input	1000	2000		

109

The table refers to the transactions of an economy in a particular year. The rows represent the sales of one sector to another and the columns what is purchased. So, in the example above, Agriculture sells $200 million worth of commodities to the Manufacturing sector in one year and $800 million to 'final demand'. Purchases by this latter category are defined as by households for consumption, by firms for investment and by government or foreigners. For simplicity of this demonstration, it is assumed here there is no foreign trade, no government purchases and no investment, implying that final demand just consists of consumption.

One of the conventions adopted is that intra-sector sales are shown as zero, i.e. the net sales inside the Agriculture sector, for example, are zero, even though the firms inside the sector sell to each other, e.g. cereals for animal feed. In this example, the sales of cereals for animal feed are subtracted from the total sales of the sector before it is recorded in the table. Hence the zeros in the table above. 'Other factor payments' are rent, interest and profit. For the latter, in the peculiar logic of capitalist financial accounting, profit is regarded as a payment by a firm for the risk taking of the owner.

The key point to notice in the table is that the sum of Agriculture's sales to Manufacturing plus other sales to final demand, is exactly the same as its purchases from manufacturing and of primary inputs. This is not accidental, and results from applying the requirement for equilibrium in an economy based on simple reproduction, where everything is consumed and nothing invested. This balance must hold for all the sectors that are included in a transaction table. The example given here is a simple version of that first developed by Leontief of the US economy. This was influenced by and used the assumptions of Marx's simple reproduction formula. However, the structure of the table is in other respects significantly different from the transaction table shown in Appendix 1, which is based on Marxist value categories.

(Presenting the results in market prices rather than using value theory does not mean though that it loses its power or usefulness in revealing the interdependencies between sectors of the economy. In fact, generally speaking, Marx's formulas analysing the capitalist system, although giving invaluable insights, are usually inappropriate when considering the workings of a planned economy. This quote from Trotsky illustrates the point, when commenting on Stalin's attempt to do this: 'Marx's formulas construct a chemically pure capitalism, which never existed and does not exist anywhere now. Precisely because of this, they reveal the basic tendencies of everyday capitalism, but precisely of capitalism and only capitalism'.[18] This quote also demonstrates that caution must also be used when applying Marx's formulas to the workings of modern capitalism. Leontief, however, avoided the potential pitfalls and successfully used Marx's theory to help develop a useful tool for planning).

To get insights into the interdependencies between sectors, it is useful as well to work out a table of Input-Output coefficients, that are calculated from the transaction table. These are obtained by dividing what one sector purchases from another by the first sector's output, which is the same as its total expenditure on inputs. For example in the table above, Manufacturing spends 200 on inputs purchased from Agriculture out of a total input of 2000, so the coefficient is 200/2000=0.1. This appears in the Manufacturing column of the Input-Output coefficient table, and a similarly calculated coefficient is put in the Agriculture column:

Input-Output Coefficient Table

	Agriculture	Manufacturing
Agriculture	0	0.1
Manufacturing	0.6	0

These coefficients can be used to answer 'what if' questions, that are useful for planning, by developing some simple equations:

Use Q_A to represent the total output of Agriculture and Q_M for Manufacturing, and use F_A and F_M to represent the final demand consumption of Agricultural and Manufacturing output. Using the logic of how the coefficients in the table above were calculated, the following equations can now be written to represent the output of each sector:

$Q_A = (0.1 \times Q_M) + F_A$
$Q_M = (0.6 \times Q_A) + F_M$

From the transaction table, if we put F_A = 800 and F_M= 1400 into these equations, we can solve them to show that Q_A =1000 and Q_M = 2000, which of course is what we already knew from the transaction table. However, if instead of doing this, we put in alternative values for F_A and F_M, we can test various hypothetical situations. For instance, we could ask the question how much a reduction of demand for agriculture commodities will cause the output of the agricultural sector to fall, if at the same time demand for manufacturing goes up. To do this, if we put in a reduced figure for F_A and an increased number for F_M, we could have for instance:

$Q_A = (0.1 \times Q_M) + 600$
$Q_M = (0.6 \times Q_A) + 1600$

now, substituting the value of Q_M from the second equation into the first gives:

$$Q_A = (0.1 \times ((0.6 \times Q_A)) + 1600) + 600$$

which gives, multiplying through: $Q_A = (0.1 \times 0.6 \times Q_A + 0.1 \times 1600) + 600 = 0.06 \times Q_A + 160 + 600$,
now bringing the Q_A terms to the left gives: $Q_A - 0.06\, Q_A = 760$. Therefore $0.94 \times Q_A = 760$,
and so $Q_A = 760/0.94 = 808.5$.

This gave the perhaps unexpected result that reducing final demand for agricultural commodities by 200 did not lead to fall of 200 in output of the sector. This was explained of course by the simultaneous increase in final demand for manufacturing, which in turn required an increase in output from Agriculture, since Manufacturing is a consumer of agricultural commodities. This simple case then demonstrates the interdependencies of industrial sectors and a way of quantifying what they are, which is potentially very powerful for planning purposes.

Also useful for planning, I/O can be used for looking at the impact of technological change on the economy. For instance, if there was a technological change in Agriculture so that it required 50% less input from Manufacturing, what would be the implications for output?

A 50% reduction in input from Manufacturing means that the coefficient in the table above, of 0.6, now becomes 0.3. Putting this value into the output equations for Q_A and Q_M gives:

$$Q_A = (0.1 \times Q_M) + F_A$$
$$Q_M = (0.3 \times Q_A) + F_M$$

From the transaction table, $F_A = 800$ and $F_M = 1400$, which gives $Q_A = 969$, and $Q_M = 1690$, when the equations are solved. The significance here is that there is a reduced requirement for agriculture, as well as manufacturing. This is because of the former's input to the latter, an outcome not necessarily immediately obvious in a more realistic situation, where many sectors are being analysed simultaneously, rather than just the two here.

For planning purposes, the most useful aspect of I/O is when the sectoral outputs are expressed in terms of the final demand. When this is done, the impact on the economy of adjusting final consumption in the different sectors, which will be decided according to social needs in a democratically planned economy, can be calculated accurately.

To demonstrate how sectoral outputs can be expressed in terms of final demand, the output equations above have to be changed round so that output is expressed just in terms of final demand. Restating our original equations:

$Q_A = (0.1 \times Q_M) + F_A$
$Q_M = (0.6 \times Q_A) + F_M$

Substituting for QA in the second equation from the first gives:

$Q_M = 0.6 \times ((0.1 \times Q_M) + F_A) + F_M = (0.06 \times Q_M) + (0.6 \times F_A) + F_M$

Subtracting 0.06 from both sides and then dividing both sides by 0.94, gives

$Q_M = 0.6383 \times F_A + 1.0638 \times F_M$

and substituting back for Q_M in the first of the original equations, gives, after re-arranging:

$Q_A = 1.0638 \times F_A + 0.1064 \times F_M$

The numbers linking the variables in these equations represent the gross output levels for each sector that correspond to unit deliveries of commodities to final demand. They appear in official statistical publications as coefficients in the following form:

Final demand commodity		
Industry	**Agriculture**	**Manufacturing**
Agriculture	1.0638	0.1064
Manufacturing	0.6383	1.0638

This table is known as a Leontief matrix, shown in a simplified form here.

If final demand, F_A and F_M, are fixed by the planners, it is simply a matter of putting the numbers into the two equations above, assuming the coefficients are known, to determine the output of a sector. This result will reflect all the industry interdependencies in a full multi-sector model and, therefore, will give a true picture of the capacity that the planners must ensure is provided in each industry, to supply a socially determined final demand. The complexity of the model will be of course vastly greater than the two sector model considered here for purposes of demonstration. For example, it could cover all the standard industrial sectors used in Britain, which are:

> Agriculture, forestry & fishing
> Mining & quarrying
> Manufacturing
> Electricity, gas & water supply
> Construction
> Distribution & hotels
> Transport & communication
> Finance & business services
> Public administration & defence
> Education, health & social work
> Other services

and that are then sub-divided into more than 100 other more detailed categories.

1. Kautsky is quoted in *The Socialist Economy, theory and practice*, by Tom Bottomore, Harvester Wheatsheaf, Hemel Hempstead, 1990, p15.
2. See Bottomore *op cit*, p26.
3. See page 511 of *Socialism: An Economic and Sociological Analysis*, by Ludwig von Mises, written in 1922, published by Jonathan Cape, London, 1936.
4. See, Paul Ekins, *'The Prospects for Green Growth'*, Routledge 2000.
5. These calculations are developed in more detail in Mandel, Chapter 16, *op cit*
6. *The Economics of Climate Change. The Stern Review*, by Nicolas Stern, Cambridge University Press, 2007
7. For an acknowledgement of his debt to Marx, see W Leontief, *Input-Output Economics 2nd edition*, Oxford University Press, Oxford, 1986.
8. For an account of Leontief's contribution to capitalist economics and an appreciation of his life from this perspective see: Baumol, W J, and T ten Raa, 'Wasily Leontief: In appreciation', *Journal of Economic and Social Measurement*, 26, (2002/2003), 1-10.
9. For a full review of the issues see: Clarke, D L, 'Planning and the Real Origins of Input-Output Analysis'. *Journal of Contemporary Asia*, 4 (4) 1984
10. For a full account of the early personal life of Leontief see: Kaliadina, S A, 'Leontief, W W and the repressions of the 1920s: an interview', *Economic Systems Research*, 18, (4), December 2006.
11. W Leontief, 'Balans naorodnovo khoziaistva SSSR-metodologicheskii razbor robotii TSSU'. *Planovoe Khoziaistva* (12), 1925, 254-258. (The balance of the economy of the USSR-a methodological critique of the work of the Central Soviet Statistical Directorate).
12. For example, see 'The Theory of Capitalist Development', by Paul Sweezy, Monthly Review Press, New York, 1968.
13. See Chapter 10 of *Marxist Economic Theory*, by Earnest Mandel, Merlin Press London, 1974.
14. W Leontief, *The Structure of the American Economy, 1919-1929*, Harvard University Press, Cambridge Mass, 1941.
15. See Clarke, D L, 'Planning and the Real Origins of Input-Output Analysis'. Journal of Contemporary Asia, op cit., for a comparison of Marx's theory and Leontief's work cited above. In this paper, Clarke compares the simple reproduction formula of Marx with the I/O analysis developed by Leontief in his original 'closed' model. In Appendix 1 of Leontief's book, 'The Structure of the American Economy', *op cit*, he puts forward the following equation relating industry outputs and inter industry flows:

$x_{31}P_1 - X_3P_3 = 0$

where X_3 represents producer goods industry output in physical terms, P_1, P_3 prices in the household and consumer goods sectors respectively, and x_{31} the flow from the producer goods sector to households. Clarke shows that X_3P_3 is equivalent to Marx's IIc and $x_{31}P_1$ to Iv + Is. In other words the formula above reduces to Marx's equilibrium requirement for simple reproduction.

16. See K Marx, *Grundrisse*. Penguin Books, 1973, p441.
17. See Chapter 16, *Marxist Economic Theory*, by Ernest Mandel, *op cit*

18. Trotsky was scathing when Stalin tried to use Marx's expanded reproduction formula to analyse the Soviet economy. See, 'Stalin as Theoretician', *Writings of Leon Trotsky (1930)*, New York, Pathfinder Press, 1975, pp326-334.
19. This example is adapted from the one put forward in Chapter 5 of Common and Stagl's book. See, Common, M and S Stagl, *Ecological Economics - An Introduction*. Cambridge University Press, Cambridge, 2005.
20. Go to this site to see a full breakdown of UK sectors used in Input Output accounting, http://www.statistics.gov.uk/downloads/theme_economy/Input_Output_Analyses_2006_edition.pdf
21. This example is given in Baumol and ten Raa, *op cit*.
22. See Chapter 9 of: Perman R, Ma Y, McGilvray J and M Common, *Natural Resource and Environmental Economics*, Pearson, 2003.

Planning for the Planet: How Socialism Could Save the Enviroment

Chapter 6:
In Defence of Socialist Planning

Ideological attacks on the concept of a socialist planned economy have taken place on theoretical as well as empirical territory, an offensive that now includes the environment. The campaign began in earnest in the 1920s, after the Russian revolution had sharpened the issues by making planning a living reality. At that time, the controversy centred around assertions that denied even the theoretical possibility of a planned economy. When this was disproved, the critics retreated to the position that a plan would be impracticable, since a modern industrial economy was too complex to be modelled and understood by any planning body. The controversies surrounding these issues came to be known as the socialist calculation debate. After this, a new empirical front was opened by the critics. They pointed to the shortcomings of the planned economy in the Soviet Union, first in a relatively muted way while the USSR was still expanding, and then after its collapse, in a barrage of propaganda.

In *Critique of the Gotha Programme*, Marx characterised the modus operandi of a fully developed socialist society in the phrase, 'from each according to ability, to each according to need'. As environmental issues have became more prominent, this aphorism has come under attack, allegedly for not recognising that there are biophysical limits to growth. Since it is most directly concerned with this book's environmental theme and is potentially the most serious of the criticisms of socialism mentioned here, this topic will be taken up first.

6.1 Socialism and the Limits to Growth

It has been argued that competitive markets degrade the environment and the alternative is a socialist society, which will be able to adopt, in its fully developed form, a sustainable economy based on collective ownership and democratic management. A socialist society as well as avoiding the waste inherent in capitalism, offers the overwhelming environmental advantage of providing conscious democratic control through planning. Democracy is not mentioned here accidentally, it is essential if planning is to be run efficiently. Lack of democracy was the main reason for the ecological devastation in the bureaucratically (mis-)planned economy of the former Soviet Union, as will be discussed later.

If conscious democratic control is the key to managing the environment, what are the pre-conditions needed to make this possible? The first, of course, is to eliminate the anarchy of the market, but just as important is to provide the mass of people with the ability to run society. Above all this means giving them the time and the knowledge to be able to participate actively in decision making. This can be done if enough leisure time is available, away from the drudgery of work, to attend meetings, and undertake educational activity and personal development. In turn, this will only be possible if there is a transformation of economic productivity so that sufficient free time is available, something requiring growth and investment. Although it might be argued that an alternative would be simply to cut production to such a level that enough leisure time would be freed up, the outcome would be counter-productive. Standards of living would fall, scarcity would increase and all the spare time created would be taken up in a battle to make up for the lost resources. It would set person against person and 'human nature' would quickly degenerate into the worst manifestations seen under capitalism. In Marx's phrase, 'all the old crap would return'. The co-operation needed, particularly internationally, to tackle the environmental crisis would be impossible.

Marx wrote in Volume 3 of *Capital* that the realm of freedom begins only where labour determined by necessity ends.[1] This means that it is necessary to satisfy all material needs in order to achieve individual freedom and it could be added now, the freedom to effectively intervene to avoid ecological breakdown. Marx considered that plenty was a necessary condition for the coming of a fully developed socialist society. Today, removing want will eliminate the causes of inequality, exploitation and conflict, and thus lay the basis for the co-operation needed for environmental regeneration. To do this will require growth.

Most Greens argue that any growth is unsustainable, and certainly not the amount needed to completely remove scarcity and want throughout the world. Marxists put the argument round the other way, that it is impossible to tackle environmental problems without effective international planning, a prerequisite for which is eliminating the conflict that results from scarcity. Satisfying needs does not mean, however, that they are infinite and will continue to expand indefinitely.

The basic needs for the majority of the world's population are stable, i.e. clothing, food, shelter, healthcare, etc., and account for the majority of consumer expenditures. In the industrialised countries, with high pressure selling and marketing, it can appear that there is an infinite demand for the latest unnecessary gizmo. However, there is actually a trend away from conspicuous consumption among the affluent middle classes, where leisure time for personal development is increasingly being put above further consumption. Under socialism, as living standards go up, free time increases dramatically and opportunities for individual development also rise, a similar trend away from commodity consumption will appear. The acquisitive habits of individuals fostered by the market economy, which are the driving force of economic behaviour in a society based on scarcity, will gradually disappear as uncertainty and worry about the future recedes and high pressure selling is removed.

These factors indicate the possibility will exist for a gradual levelling off of consumption, albeit at a higher level than exists today, into a steady state equilibrium. It is impossible to define exactly what this higher equilibrium level of consumption will be. It will depend on a multitude of unpredictable factors, not least how quickly human psychology adjusts to the new conditions. It is theoretically possible that in the industrialised countries quality of life can be increased significantly for everyone in the transitional period, without further large increases in consumption. This would be possible with the benefits of democratic socialist planning, after the elimination of capitalist duplication and waste and with the other advantages of socialism already discussed. However, for the majority of the world's population in the ex-colonial world, significant rises in consumption will be needed to meet basic needs. For a harmonious, efficient, socialist system to exist, the entire population of the planet must have comparable standards of living, which means that the level of consumption in the industrialised world must apply to everyone. This will require a massive reduction of environmental intensity for sustainability, if projections of big population increases are still used (see Chapter 3 Appendix, for some detailed examples).

The size of this task could be mitigated if the projection is not borne out that population in the 'South' will continue increasing rapidly, because there is a clear relationship between falling population growth and increases in consumption. This was found to be true even in countries where standards of living were relatively low, such as the former Soviet Bloc. In democratic socialist societies, as well as increases in consumption, there will be a growing sense of security and solidarity (in contrast to the former Soviet Union). This is another factor that will tend to lessen the perceived need for the 'protection' of big families. In addition, access by women to education, good jobs and the provision of free contraception will reduce the growth of population. So, if current projections of population increases are not reached under socialism, the scale of the environmental problem will correspondingly fall.

Recognising that the rate of population growth may fall does not endorse population control, advocated by some Greens as a way out of the crisis, or put the blame for environmental problems on alleged overpopulation. Marx, attacked Malthus's ideas on overpopulation. He said that rather than being subject to some supra-historical natural law, the level of population was 'a historically determined relation, in no way determined by abstract numbers or by the absolute limit of the productivity of the necessaries of life, but by the limits posited rather by *specific conditions of production*' (Marx's emphasis). He went on, 'How small do the numbers which meant overpopulation for the Athenians appear to us!'[2] Marx and Engels, of course, were extremely hostile to Malthus, Marx calling his ideas a libel on the human race since they blamed the poor for their poverty. Later, Engels indignantly refuted attempts to use Malthusian arguments to justify Social Darwinism.[3] Marx pointed out in *Grundrisse* that Malthus conjured his idea out of thin air. There was no evidence that population was destined to grow at an exponential rate and food production only linearly, leading to eternally re-occurring famines, for which the poor had only themselves to blame. Following classical economic theory, Engels and subsequently Lenin, showed that although food production was subject to a law of diminishing returns, this meant production could be increased using advances in technology and science. It was not therefore subject to the supra-historical natural law that Malthus was claiming.[4] This outcome has clearly been confirmed by history. Also, Malthus's idea of population increasing exponentially, following a similar natural law, has been refuted by history with birth rates falling sharply in industrialised countries.

Despite the discrediting of his ideas, many Greens, including some on the Left, continue to believe his theories. Some have already jumped in with alarmist and inflammatory prognostications, such as that by James Lovelock, the promoter of the Gaia environmental theory. He was quoted in the *Guardian* as saying 'we should call a halt to all immigration or encourage people to go abroad....I see us as a lifeboat with the person in charge saying, "We can't take any more or else we'll sink"' (14/1/11). Others, like George Monbiot, while rejecting the over-population scare, put the blame for the looming environmental catastrophe on excessive consumption by the industrialised 'rich' nations. Blaming over consumption or over population for the environmental crisis is missing the point. Famine and malnutrition where they occur, are the products of a dysfunctional socio-economic system, i.e. capitalism and its colonialist legacy, not too many people. Also, putting Lovelock's 'full-up' idea into perspective, the entire population of the world will fit into the Los Angeles metropolitan area, albeit shoulder to shoulder, according to the *Guardian* article cited above.

Leaving aside humanitarian considerations, population control methods advocated by some Greens are counter-productive because they inevitably instil enormous hostility against the state by the very poor. They frustrate efforts to build the human solidarity necessary for the socialist project. Where such schemes have been imposed by governments, they have led to near-insurrection followed by collapse, as in India under Indira Gandhi in the 1970s. It is true that in China the 'one-child policy' was associated with a birth rate lower than in India, but to what extent population control policy was responsible for the relatively lower birth rate is not clear. Other factors were also in play in checking population growth, such as rising per capita incomes and growing urbanisation. Even if population control measures did have an effect, they occurred in the context of extreme repression by a ruthless and dictatorial Stalinist regime and were not accompanied by any improvement in environmental conditions – just the opposite.

In a socialist state, the scale of the ecological challenge will also be reduced by redistribution of wealth from the super rich, who use a disproportionate share of resources (e.g. for private jets) compared to the rest of society. Since the rich absorb 5% of output, eliminating their consumption will make a small, but significant difference. While this, and the possibility of lower than expected population increases will mitigate the problem of reducing pollution, the size of the task will still be big. It will require a transformation of current patterns of energy and resource use, so that environmental intensity is reduced massively.

Most Greens will argue that since such a reduction in environmental intensity is impossible, the increase in consumption by everyone on the planet, along the lines proposed here, will be unsustainable and go beyond the biophysical limits of the globe to maintain life. This position is held also by the vast majority of eco-socialists and 'eco-Marxists', (see box on Eco-socialism).

Eco-socialism

Eco-socialism is still marginalised in the Green movement, but as the total inability of capitalist solutions to solve environmental problems become more apparent, interest in it will inevitably grow. Eco-socialists share many of the criticisms made here of market-led environmentalism. At the same time most, but not all, reject the possibility of growth in consumption due to the assumed bio-physical limits of the earth's resources. They therefore advocate a steady state economy, usually starting from a lower base of consumption, although exactly what this should be is often left vague. In this context, Marx is often criticised by eco-socialists both for his ideas on 'super-abundance' and because his thought, in particular his economic value theory, did not encompass an environmental dimension. For example, the prominent 'eco-Marxist', James O'Connor writes:

'Marx never put two and two together to argue that "natural" barriers may be capitalistically produced barriers. In other words there may be a contradiction of capitalism which leads to an "ecological" theory of crisis and social transformation'.[6]

The issue of super-abundance has already been taken up in the discussion on the limits to growth, but the other questions will be be answered here. Marx's discovery of the laws of capital accumulation and expanded reproduction, discussed earlier, pointed to capitalism's need for permanent growth in order to maintain profits in a competitive market - an insight of great value in the green debate today. The implication of this theory, in answer to O'Connor's point, is that an ecological crisis could eventually emerge under certain circumstances. In the middle of the 19th Century the level of pollution was a fraction of that today, and a threat to sustainability on a world scale did not exist. In this concrete context, Marx correctly argued that there were no natural barriers to plenty and abundance, in answer to Malthus' idea that generalised poverty was an inevitable and permanent feature of the human condition

More broadly speaking, it is not true to say that Marx and Engels' theories did not contain an environmental dimension or were incompatible with the need to address environmental questions. At a high level of generalisation Marx's simultaneous emphasis on social and material factors in his analysis of the market economy, in terms of values and use-values (labour and commodities), gives a good point of departure for further consideration of environmental relations. More concretely, Engels made some telling remarks on the impact of capitalism on the environment and the fundamentally dependent relations between humankind and the natural world in *The Part Played by Labour in the Transition from Ape to Man*. For example, '...at every step we are reminded that that we by no means rule over nature like a conqueror of a foreign people, like someone standing outside nature, but we belong to nature and stand in its midst.' And later: 'after the mighty advances made by natural sciences in the present century, we are more than ever in a position to ...control... our day to day production activities. But the more this progresses, the more will men not only feel but also know their oneness with nature'.[7]

The most positive aspect of the development of the eco-socialist movement is that planning is now being seriously debated as a tool to organise production. The debate includes the possible danger of the degeneration of a future planned socialist society into a totalitarian state, as in the Soviet Union. This serious discussion of planning in environmental circles, is a harbinger of a wider debate that will develop in the anti-capitalist movement in the next few years. As this discussion develops, it is important to understand the implications for future society of what many eco-socialists are saying about the requirement for massive cuts in consumption.

Some supporters of eco-socialism advocate a cut in consumption of 10 times, including massive cuts in the Third World.[8] The political form such a society would take, with a material basis at a feudal or pre-feudal level, would be eco-Stalinist, a totalitarian police state that would make Stalin's Russia seem benign. To talk about such a society being based on fairness and equality is a mockery, although to be fair, some of its advocates are honest enough to concede that repressive measures may be necessary. (Ironically, this nightmare regime would probably not even have sufficient resources to operate the apparatus of a police state necessary to maintain itself in power.) How such an eco-society, based on near subsistence consumption, could come about is left somewhat vague by its advocates, which is not surprising since it is hard to see who it would appeal to. The mostly unspoken perspective is that it will emerge after a collapse of the present world order, due to environmental catastrophe. Even this hope is probably forlorn, since such a state would adopt some pre-capitalist form of organisation, corresponding to its low material base, meaning the whole rotten cycle would begin again.

It is true that there may be bio-physical limits, including ultimately, in the abstract, for population, but it is impossible to say what exactly they are. Bio-physical limits will depend, amongst other things, on the possibilities of substituting with renewables and introducing new technology to increase productivity. (There is a theory developed from the Second Law of Thermodynamics, which is popular with environmentalists,[5] that claims to show that all human activity generates irreversible increases in 'entropy' or ecological disorder. This leads eventually to environmental breakdown. The empirical evidence to back up the theory is limited. In particular it does not predict concretely what the limits to growth are, apart from stating that they theoretically exist.) Whether a natural limit to human resource use exists is not however the issue. It is not proposed to increase consumption unsustainably, rather to transform resource use with socialist methods. In as concrete terms as possible, this book has tried to outline the ways this could be achieved.

6.2. Technical objections to planned economy

As was to be expected for a revolutionary theory that threatened the foundations of capitalist society, objections to Marx's ideas were common virtually from the time the ink was dry on the first volume of *Capital*. However, detailed critiques of how a socialist society would function did not emerge until after it became a living issue following the Russian Revolution of 1917. The academic standard bearers of the critics were Ludwig von Mises and Frederick von Hayek. They focussed on how economic calculation proceeds in a planned economy, in particular in determining prices. This led von Mises to take the position that any planned socialist society was a theoretical impossibility, illustrated by his apocalyptic visions of the resulting wasteland quoted in Chapter 5.

To follow the arguments it is necessary to look into the background in some detail. When capitalism has been replaced and a plan installed, it will be necessary to meet needs on a world scale. As well as addressing the other priorities for socialism, this will be required to permit the meaningful international cooperation necessary to tackle global warming (see 6.1 above). The context in which this is done will remain one of relative scarcity inherited from capitalism. Dealing with scarcity, although declining as output increases, will need a system of resource allocation. The most efficient mechanism for this will be the retention of money as a medium of exchange. Further, to smooth the transition to a fully developed socialist society, most Marxists in the past, including Lenin and Trotsky[9] have recognised the need to retain market mechanisms for the production of consumer goods, whilst producers' goods would be planned.

To what extent this rule of thumb will apply in a future socialist society cannot be determined in advance, it will depend on the circumstances. For example, consumers goods today are often produced by multinational corporations, using extensive and sophisticated planning techniques to coordinate their operations across the globe. This is particularly the case in car manufacture, where it would clearly be ridiculous to break up and abandon the extensive planning already in use. What would be needed is to integrate the operations of the handful of existing firms into a worldwide plan of production, democratically organised and with an environmental dimension.

In some circumstances it may not be possible to integrate production on a world scale in the short term, due to the frictions of the transition process, and it may be necessary then to contemplate more extensive use of market approaches. In particular, this could be the case if capitalism is not replaced first in the industrialised advanced economies. It is clear that there are many imponderables to wrestle with that cannot be addressed in advance and involves a whole new debate. To answer the critics who ask what would happen if planning had to be introduced in unfavourable circumstances, let us assume that in some form a division will exist between consumer and capital goods.

If we assume for the sake of argument that consumer goods will be priced according to market supply and demand, how then can prices be determined for capital goods that reflect real costs of production, without which efficient planning is impossible? As von Mises put it: 'Where there is no free market, there is no pricing mechanism; without a pricing mechanism, there is no economic calculation'?[10] Historically, this challenge was taken up by the Marxist economists, Lange and Taylor,[11] with others. They proposed constructing an artificial competitive market in producers' (capital) goods to allow prices to be formed for the purposes of accounting (see the Appendix on the 'socialist calculation' controversy).

Lange and Taylor's system for a planned economy, although viable, included serious potential problems, explained in the Appendix, linked to the operation of the laws of supply and demand. The compromises with the market that Lange and Taylor thought necessary, were linked to the then technology and relatively backward conditions of the 1930s. They developed their pseudo-market approach in response to criticisms of the complexity of planning, summed up in the following quote from a leading co-thinker of Hayek, Lionel Robbins: 'On paper we can conceive their problem to be solved by a series of mathematical calculations....But in practice, this solution is quite unworkable. It would necessitate the drawing up of millions of equations on the basis of millions of statistical data based on many more millions of individual computations. By the time the equations were solved, the information on which they were based would have become obsolete and they would need to be recalculated anew.'[18] The technological possibilities that now exist to obtain the necessary data input for a plan and to rapidly reprocess them, summarised in Chapter 5, clearly answer the points made by Robbins.

In the future it would not necessarily be the case that a pseudo-market system would have to be adopted. The starting point for a plan of production could be historically given prices, as with Lange and Taylor's scheme. Then, rather than proceed by way of a pseudo-market, inputs to the plan that reflected the real state of the economy, with its constantly changing tastes and needs, could be determined analytically. This would be made possible by the following factors: the quality and breadth of the information available through modern communication systems, the sophisticated planning tools available, such I/O analysis, and crucially, by the checks and balances provided by democratic institutions of consumers and producers.

As discussed earlier, since it is impossible to predict the exact circumstances accompanying the introduction of socialism, it is necessary to answer the critics who ask what would happen if there were less than favourable conditions. In such a theoretical case, it may not be possible to analytically generate some data for the plan. This could be due to the dislocations and difficulties of the transition period, where modern technology is temporarily unavailable, for example. This will not preclude creating a plan of production, it would just require the construction of a pseudo-market, along Lange and Taylor's lines, to facilitate the determination of real prices of production. If this had to be done, particular vigilance would be necessary to guard against the dangers inherent in such an approach, discussed in the Appendix.

What would need to remain of Lange and Taylor's system would be the central idea of incorporating true prices of production in the plan. These would have to be regularly updated, whilst recognising that prices will have to vary for certain periods of time from the 'real' price, to fulfil social needs. As mentioned in the Appendix, this process needs to be carefully monitored and controlled so that serious distortions in the pricing structure do not appear, and a rational balance is maintained between plan and market. A balance also needs to be struck between demands of centralisation and decentralisation when the plan is implemented at enterprise level. The workers at the shop floor need to feel they have a stake in production, which will require a certain level of autonomy for the enterprises. At the same time, all production units must ultimately be subject to the plan and its democratically determined priorities.

Of course, the need to incentivise staff will decline as a socialist consciousness grows in the new society, but in the transition there will be a tension. Too much decentralisation and the dangers increase of competition growing between autonomous production units, to the extent that a return to the negative features of the market economy is threatened. Such a development could be driven by managers of enterprises operating increasingly in their own interests. On the other hand, over-centralised planning can reinforce bureaucratic tendencies by the state to dominate the economy, alienating workers and consumers in the process. This could lead to a central apparatus acting in its own interest and not that of society. As we will see below from the experience of the Soviet Union, these are very real dangers to the socialist project, far greater than any technical problems with planning systems. The only way to combat the dangers is to ensure democratic bodies are established to exercise real control at all levels, and that their independence is effectively guarded.

6.3 Lessons of the Soviet Union

The final redoubt of the critics of a socialist planned economy is to highlight the experience of the Soviet Union. Notwithstanding the technical merits or demerits of planning systems, the objectors claim that the Soviet experience proved 'real life socialism' did not work. In particular, Greens sceptical of central planning point to the environmental devastation wreaked on the USSR by its rulers. To answer the critics requires a brief account of Soviet history and drawing from this, how the problems it encountered could have been avoided.

The Russian Revolution

Since the collapse of the USSR, the academics have been busily rewriting history. One of the myths now being put forward is that capitalism before 1917 was developing rapidly and successfully and the revolution in that year cut across this. It is true that there was a feverish growth of industry in a few big cities in the Czarist empire (the Czar was the autocratic ruler of the Russian empire, which stretched from Poland to Alaska) Growth had an unbalanced and convulsive character, which depended on the profits generated by impoverished and super-oppressed workers herded into massive factories. There was a complete failure by the new capitalist class to transform the country into a modern industrialised society. In particular, it remained dominated by neo-feudal landlords, ruling over an exploited peasantry, who were only recently released from serfdom. There was no sign of the development of an efficient agricultural sector run on capitalist lines, capable of supporting wide-scale urban industry. Also, crucially, the oppression of the non-Russian peoples of the empire continued unabated during the late nineteenth and early twentieth centuries and resulted in a seething discontent - a bomb ticking away.

These factors undermined the stability of the system and created the conditions for the revolution, the trigger being the horrific conditions resulting from the First World War, where millions of peasants were slaughtered in the trenches and the countryside gradually bled to death. The socialist revolution of October 1917, led by Lenin and Trotsky, was unique because it was the first time that the capitalist system had been overthrown and a workers' state established. It was based on soviets, committees of workers and soldiers created spontaneously during the course of the revolution to organise activity, that were later to become the organs through which the new society would be built. Initially the soviets were democratic bodies where strict controls were imposed on elected representatives to prevent them usurping their positions.

The degeneration of the revolution

The successful overthrow of capitalism in Russia engendered the wrath of the ruling classes throughout the world, resulting in a cruel and bloody civil war where millions died and the country was devastated. All the main Western countries, including Britain and the USA, sent armies into the country to aid the pro-Czarist forces trying to overthrow the new socialist government. However, the world's first workers' state emerged victorious due to the heroism and self-sacrifice of the Russian workers and peasants trying to build a new society. Victory would have been much more difficult if the Bolshevik government had not had the support of workers in the West, because the main powers dared not intervene more widely because of fear of provoking indignation and revolution in their own countries.

Victory was won at a price since the best and most class conscious workers were killed in the war, meaning that it became easier for careerist and corrupt elements to infiltrate the soviets and ultimately take them over. This process was accelerated by the terrible conditions facing Russia, ravaged by famine and disease and devastated by the economic dislocation resulting from the First World War and the civil war. It took years of back-breaking effort to re-organise society just to get it back to the pre-war level. In these appalling circumstances of a struggle to survive, speculators and careerists prospered and each began to look for ways to build their political influence. Gradually the lower ranks of the soviets came under their control as they formed alliances with demoralised workers' leaders, and they then looked for support higher up in the bureaucracy that was emerging. They found what they were after in the person of Joseph Stalin, originally a minor figure in the revolution. He was hungry for personal power and saw a chance to consolidate his position by allying himself with the new layer of corrupt bureaucrats. As a result, by the late 1920s, all vestiges of democracy had been removed from Soviet society by Stalin and his supporters, despite a heroic effort by the socialists around Leon Trotsky to defend the democratic principles of the October revolution.

Was this degeneration inevitable as the critics hostile to socialism claim, implying that the revolution itself was counter-productive and futile? Lenin, the leader of the revolution, had no illusions of the difficulties facing the Bolshevik government. His belief was that a revolution in Russia would be part of a European wide movement of the working class to overthrow their oppressors. When the opportunity arose to take power in October 1917, he had no hesitation in pressing forward, even though the poverty and backwardness in Russia made for a very difficult environment to build socialism. Lenin correctly foresaw that Europe was a powder keg, due to the conditions created by the world war. A successful uprising in Russia would be a spur to workers in other more developed countries, like Germany, to take power. When this happened the German workers would come to the aid of their comrades in Russia and ease the difficulties they faced, enabling a healthy democratic workers state to be built. This perspective answered the argument of the right wing workers' leaders, who used Marx's writings to oppose the revolution. He had envisaged socialism first starting in the most advanced capitalist country, not the most backward. (In his later writings, Marx did though pose the possibility of a revolution in Russia.)

Lenin was proved right in predicting revolutionary turmoil throughout Europe as a result of the Russian revolution and the effects of the imperialist world war. Unfortunately all these attempts to overthrow capitalism were unsuccessful, due partly to the mistakes and inexperience of the revolutionary workers, but mainly to the betrayals of the leaders of the European social democratic parties and trades unions. This failure was not inevitable or preordained, the outcome could only be determined by the course of the struggle itself. Particularly in Germany, the situation had been on a knife-edge. Nevertheless, the result was that the world's first workers' state was left isolated and impoverished. This development allowed the layer of demoralised and corrupt bureaucrats to consolidate their position. By this time, only the intervention and help of the international working class, with its democratic traditions, would have been capable of dislodging them. The wiping out of the remnants of democratic workers control of society by the new bureaucratic caste was ultimately to lead to the collapse of the Soviet Union.

The five year plan

In the early twenties, the new government in Russia had been forced to re-introduce a widespread capitalist market in order to revive the economy from the devastation inflicted on it. This successfully boosted food production but at the same time created a new class of rich farmers called kulaks. The socialist opponents of Stalin, particularly Leon Trotsky, warned that the kulaks' economic power would eventually grow to such an extent that they would threaten the regime. Stalin ignored this warning, but panicked when the danger was imminent in the late 1920s. He then took drastic steps to transform the country from a predominantly agricultural to an industrial society. A five year plan was introduced to build up heavy industry at a breakneck speed and a programme of repression implemented to 'liquidate the kulaks as a class'. The new line was given an ideological cover under the slogan of building 'socialism in one country', i.e. a conscious rejection of the internationalism that up to then had been at the heart of socialist thinking.

Much to Stalin's surprise, the results of the drive to industrialise the country were spectacular and growth targets had to be raised every few months as production exceeded the plan. Within a decade, the Soviet Union was an industrial giant rivalling the capitalist powers. How was this achieved? The first point to make is that the transformation was unprecedented in history. The capitalist countries had taken centuries of development to get to this point. The driving force in Russia was the plan of production itself. Freed from the shackles of the market system, then in its deepest crisis after the Wall Street crash, there seemed to be no limit to growth. The allocation of resources directly by the state planning body, rather than by the 'hidden hand' of market forces, ensured that the pace of growth was staggering.

There was, however, a downside to the economic miracle. There was huge wastage; up to 30% of production, due to the bungling, corruption and bad planning inherent in the undemocratic command system of economic management. The quality of goods was bad; Trotsky called poor quality the Achilles Heel of the planned economy.[15] The only way to get round this problem was to introduce a democratic system of control over production, where consumers and workers would have real power to ensure that the goods produced were both fit for purpose and made in the right quantities. The re-introduction of the soviets on democratic lines could have achieved this. But Stalin would not contemplate such a course, because any vestige of democracy would have threatened his regime, which despite the calm on the surface was unstable. It should not be forgotten that much of the new infrastructure to support industry was built by armies of slave labour political prisoners, where millions perished due to the fiendish conditions imposed on them. The survivors of the camps and the super-exploited workers would have taken a swift revenge if Stalin had loosened the noose for a moment.

Where did it go wrong?

The resilience of the planning system was demonstrated again after the Second World War when society was rapidly rebuilt after being virtually demolished by the Nazi rampage. By the 1960s, the Soviet Union was at its peak, a pioneer of space travel, a superpower rivalled only by the USA. The statistics below demonstrate the economic situation at that time.

The first table shows that in the production of basic industrial commodities, the USSR was in the same league as the main capitalist powers, although it never managed to overtake the USA. The second table, however, gives a more contradictory picture as far as consumer goods are concerned. For simple goods, e.g. footware, there was comparability. In technology based industries, like artificial fibres there was a huge gap, which continued to increase over the next 25 years.

Table 1: Production per head of Population 1964

	France	Italy	Britain	W. Germany	USA	USSR
Electric Power (kwh)	2051	1474	3418	2835	5984	2013
Sulphuric Acid (kg)	56	54	59	62	108	34
Cement (kg)	448	436	315	579	319	285

Table 2: Consumption per head of Population 1962-3

	USSR	USA	Britain	France
Meat (kg)	39	85	71	78
Artificial textiles (kg)	1.6	6.7	6.3	5.0
Leather Shoes	2.1	3.7	2.8	2.3

(Source: E Mandel, *Marxist Economic Theory*, Merlin Press 1968, p558)

The second table also shows that the production of food lagged behind, a legacy of the mayhem that resulted from the forced collectivisation of agriculture in the 1930s - a disaster the USSR never recovered from. Despite the problems, in the 1960s it still appeared that the Soviet Union was on course to overtake the West. Indeed, after the Soviet leader Khruschev boasted about this, the then British Prime Minister, Macmillan, commissioned a secret report to see if was possible. The research concluded that, on the basis of the available evidence, it could happen.

History showed that the gap between the West and the USSR gradually increased from the 1960s, and by the 1980s the Soviet economy was at a standstill. How can this be explained? There were two fundamental interlinked factors involved: the inability of undemocratic bureaucratic planning to cope with the needs of a modern, technology-based consumer society and the failure of the command system of industrial management. Consider the second first. During the Stalin period the bureaucrats were subjected to a 'carrot and stick' approach, where they were richly rewarded for reaching the planning targets but subject to fierce reprisals if they failed (one of the aims of the Great Purges of the 30s was to terrorise this group). This approach worked in the early period, from both points of view. The material incentives were massive, particularly since the bureaucrats were starting from a very low base, and the fear factor was palpable.

By the 1960s, however, the repression had eased following Stalin's death and the material incentive was less strong, since the bureaucrats already had an opulent lifestyle. The managers were content to sit back and enjoy life; their main priority was to defend their privileges. The development of the economy was of minor concern for them. A particularly damaging result of the indifference of the bureaucrats to the harmonious development of society was the degeneration of the environment that became increasingly serious (see box on Soviet environment).

The destruction of the environment in the Soviet Union

The destruction of the environment in the Ukraine after the Chernobyl disaster was the most shocking example of preventable damage to nature in the Soviet Union, but it was only one disaster out of many. Towards the end of the USSR a whistle blower smuggled a book to the West that painted a frightening picture of the damage caused by bureaucratic indifference.[16] The book revealed the huge gap between the protection theoretically provided by the law in environmental questions and the reality, as was the case in other aspects of life under Stalinism. As the author correctly stated, the existence of a plan of production should have meant that Russia was in the forefront of environmental protection and workers' health and safety. The reality was totally divorced from the hypocritical claims of the rulers in the Kremlin to lead the world in this area.

In the large city of Donetsk, in the mining region of the south, lung cancer rates among the general population were 300% above average due to air pollution. In

Leninogorsk, a city of 100,000 in Kazakhstan, the concentration of lead in the air was measured at 440 times above the maximum permissible level. There is a well established link between such pollution and brain damage in children, and dozens of similar cases were reported in the book. The Soviet magazine, Sanitation and Health, quoted in the book, reported that 50% of the male population in Tatarsk in Siberia suffered from impotence due to the high level of the metal boron in the water supply. The blustering and demagogy of the top leadership in the Soviet Union made matters worse. Khruschev, who was the General Secretary of the 'Communist' Party in the 50 and 60s, set up a campaign to drain 10 million hectares (about 30,000 square miles) of swampland to make agriculture more productive. This proved to be disastrous since the project consumed enormous resources. All the experts involved knew that it would result in turning the swamps into deserts due to soil erosion. No-one dared contradict the 'Great Leader', with the result that over one million square miles suffered soil erosion, which represented nearly half of all agricultural land.

The rapacious life style of the bureaucrats also threatened endangered species, due the indiscriminate slaughter they committed on their hunting expeditions. When Marshall Batitskii, commander of the Soviet strategic missile forces, organised a hunt of polar bears in 1976 he made sure the odds were heavily stacked in his favour by firing from a specially converted helicopter with a machine gun. Not to be outdone, some of his subordinates stationed near Lake Baikal, in Siberia, decided to make absolutely sure of success in their battle with the wild by employing heat-seeking ground-to-ground guided missiles.

The author made the point that 'wherever one traces the thread of ecology, it always leads deep into the social and economic structure of society'. By this, it was clear that he meant the role in society played by the bureaucracy who did not suffer from the same ecological and pollution problems as the overwhelming majority of the population. As a result, he was not hopeful that any reform of the system would be possible. The author didn't make the general conclusion though, that the destruction of the environment and the systematic poisoning of the population was a direct result of bureaucratic misrule.

Another interlinked reason contributing to the economic decline was the first factor mentioned above, the breakdown of the planning system. In the first period of Soviet development, the task was to develop basic industries and infrastructure, relatively simple from a planning point of view. There was huge wastage because of the undemocratic methods employed, but the inherent advantages of planning over the market meant that the results were still initially dramatically successful. There was also an ample supply of labour available from the peasantry - most of the economic growth was due to putting these people into the labour force. After the basic industries were built, however, the job was to orientate the economy to the mass production of consumer goods, a task that involved increasing the productivity of labour by applying modern technology. This is more complicated from a planning point of view, but by the 1960s new planning techniques were available using computers which would have made this technically possible.

However, the potential problems outlined in the previous section with regard to planning now became even more of a incubus on the system. The more complicated an economy, the more it needs continuous checking and revision. The opaqueness of the pricing system that had existed since the earliest five-year plan now became even more of a problem. Initially, the planning bodies fixed 'real' prices, to which they added a 'turnover tax' at levels that varied according to particular goods. Alternatively, they may have imposed a subsidy. This was meant to encourage the use of production methods with a high capital component, whereas the 'turnover tax' provided the resources needed for investment, at the expense of consumers.

The problem was that following inflation, upheavals in agriculture and repeated arbitrary changes in prices, the planning authorities no longer knew what the real costs of production were. The result was that the distortions that had always existed in the economy became worse. It was impossible to rationally decide on the investments needed to fulfil a particular social priority. What was also missing was the essential element of democratic control in the allocation of resources, where the needs of consumers must be fed back to the planning bodies and acted upon. Since the bureaucrats were unaccountable to the consumer, and indifferent to their needs, for the reasons discussed above, nothing happened. As a result the economy went into a long term decline and came to a halt almost completely in the mid 1980s.

The collapse of the Soviet Union

The effect of the economic stagnation was a demoralisation of large sections of the ruling caste and some of them began to consider a move to capitalism. Many were particularly demoralised by the failure of the USSR to match the advances in military related technology that had been achieved by the USA. The technological gap between the two countries that had almost closed in the 1950s and 1960s now became a chasm. It was particularly marked in the key areas of electronics, computers, automation and advanced materials.[17]

Gorbachev, the Soviet leader from the mid-1980s, still believed that reform of the system was possible, by bringing in elements of the market and decentralisation to make the command economy work more efficiently. He did this by giving the Soviet republics huge powers to make autonomous decisions, a policy that unwittingly led to political disintegration very rapidly. This was due to an explosive growth of nationalism, suppressed during the Soviet period, but not eliminated. The process proved unstoppable and the Soviet Union, the first workers' state, collapsed ignominiously. Capitalism, with all its horrors, emerged from the ashes.

This historical defeat for the working class can be traced back to the eradication of democracy in the Soviet political system in the 1920s. In turn, this lead to economic failure, to political counter-revolution and ultimately to collapse. The failure of the USSR was not a failure of socialism. Genuine socialism must be based on a non-capitalist planned economy. It has also to be linked, to function efficiently, to democratic controls at all levels of society, a requirement that was not met in Russia. Even if it is accepted that democracy in a planned system is vital if it is to work effectively, the critics may still say that the degeneration of the revolution was inevitable. It is argued here that this was not the case. Although poverty and backwardness in Russia created fertile ground for Stalinist totalitarianism, the international movement that the events of 1917 triggered could have cut across this development. The working class in an advanced country like Germany could have taken power and coming to the aid of their Russian comrades. This outcome, which was in the balance, would have made a decisive difference and resulted in history taking a completely different course.

Appendix:

The 'socialist calculation' controversy

After first denying it, Hayek subsequently acknowledged the theoretical possibility of planning, although von Mises was still reluctant.[12] Hayek then retreated to the position that in practice planning would be impossible to achieve. Prices are formed and are constantly changing, as a result of the independent decisions of thousands of producers, or in the case of consumers, millions. Hence it could require the solution of millions of equations to arrive at a plan.

Lange and Taylor's response was to put forward a system using historically given prices as a starting point, and then using a process of trial and error to arrive at a real cost of production. In doing this, they first made the point that producers and consumers in a market economy, at any given moment, treat prices they face as fixed, or immutable (disregarding the odd market trader who is still willing to haggle), so dramatically simplifying the calculation. If these historically given prices, which are then used, and must be treated as fixed by plant managers and consumers, are not 'real' (i.e. not equal to the marginal cost, using neo-classical categories, or prices of production in Marxist terms), then a glut or deficit will develop. This would cause production to go up or down according to whether prices are above or below marginal cost. In turn, prices would adjust up or down to bring supply and demand into equilibrium and after a few such cycles, a 'real' equilibrium price would emerge. In such a process, it would be plant managers who would be obliged by the planners to adjust output to achieve equilibrium prices, as opposed to the 'hidden hand' of a true market.

This in essence was a system of market socialism that got round the technical objections of Hayek and von Mises. Incidentally, on Hayek's original objection about the impossibility of determining price from the actions of millions of consumers, modern techniques can now monitor the purchases by consumers on an individual basis for the purpose of marketing, as we saw in Chapter 5. Another refutation of the alleged impossibility of planning is, of course, the example of planned economy in the Soviet Union. The USSR, despite its profound problems, existed for more than 60 years and achieved a transformation of a massive country into an industrial society unprecedented in its scope and speed.

One comment of Hayek however did have some truth, which was that the adoption of Lange and Taylor's pseudo-market system would have meant the claimed superiority of planning over competition was abandoned. It is true that as described, market socialism could have reproduced some of the negative features of capitalism, and risked throwing the baby out with the bath water. For instance, as prices were constantly adjusted due to changing consumer preferences and technological change, an information lag would develop, with prices necessarily changed always after the event.[14] This could have lead to wastage of perishable goods or, for example, to the phenomenon of overproduction, seen with the 'blind', autonomous, capitalist market. Today this criticism has less weight than at the time of the original controversy, since information is almost instantaneously available with modern communication systems in advanced industrial societies.

The real problem with a system that adheres to equilibrium prices is that social priorities, democratically decided by the mass of the people, could play second fiddle to the dictates of 'supply and demand'. To avoid this will mean the abandonment of certain equilibrium prices if they conflict with achieving these democratically decided social needs. For example, if the operation of the plan was not having the effect of reducing unemployment in a particular part of the country, or of achieving environmental goals, then equilibrium prices would have to be abandoned and a planning directive made to allocate resources into the necessary areas.

Taking this course of action is not without dangers to the healthy functioning of a planned economy. If taken too far, it can lead to a potentially dangerously obscure pricing system developing, which could undermine the efficient operation of the plan. This was certainly the case in the former Soviet Union, where the problem was vastly compounded because political and economic priorities were bureaucratically and arbitrarily imposed rather than democratically decided. This led to distortions which could not be corrected, because there was no democratically accountable body able to monitor and control the pricing system for the general good.

There is inevitably a tension between socially determined needs and the requirement to maintain equilibrium prices. In fact, there can be no true market for capital goods and therefore real market prices, without autonomous competing producers. If the latter is contemplated, then the tension will be resolved in the direction of a return to a capitalist system. The superiority of a socialist planned economy, however, is that it substitutes the concept of maximum overall efficiency of investment by the community for the concept of profit maximisation by each enterprise. It follows that under socialism, if necessary to fulfil social needs, certain individual enterprises could be obliged to make a loss.

1   K Marx, *Capital*, Volume 3, Harmondsworth, Penguin, 1981, pp 958-9.
2   Quote from K Marx, *Grundrisse*, Harmondsworth, Penguin, 1973, pp605-606.
3   Marx attacking Malthus in letter to J B Schweitzer, in Karl Marx and Frederick Engels, *Selected Works*, Vol. 2, Progress Publishers, Moscow, 1969, p24, and Engels in a letter to Lavrov on Social Darwinism in Marx Engels, *Selected Works*, *op cit.*, Vol 3, p 478.
4   For a summary of the arguments see, *Marx and Engels on Malthus*, Edited by R L Meek, London, Lawrence and Wishart, 1953.
5   Georgescu-Roegen, N, 'The entropy law and the economic process in retrospect' *Eastern Economic Journal*, Jan-Mar 1986. For a critique, albeit from a post-modernist perspective, see: Luks F, 'Deconstructing economic interpretations of sustainable development: Limits, scarcity and abundance'. In, Ed. L Mehta, *The Limits to Scarcity*, London Earthscan, 2010.
6   O'Connor is quoted in *Eco-capitalism or eco-socialism*, by Saral Sarkar, London, Zed books, 1999, p199.
7   Both quotes are from *Part Played by Nature in the Transition from Ape to Man*, by Frederick Engels, Marx Engels, *Selected Works*, Vol 3, *op cit*, pp74-75.
8   Some who are advocating this, such as Saral Sarkar, in *Eco-capitalism or eco-socialism, op cit.*, are frank enough to admit that such cuts in consumption would be not be consistent with creating any form of socialist society based on Marx's ideas. He criticises other eco-socialists who, while rejecting the possibility of very significantly reducing energy intensity, do not face up to the consequent need to cut consumption by the massive amounts required to address environmental threats.
9   See the *The Tax in Kind*, by V I Lenin, go to: www.marxist.org/archive/lenin/works/1921/apr/21.htm and *Stalin as Theoretician*, by L D Trotsky, go to: www.marxist.org/archive/trotsky/1930/03/stalin.htm
10 Von Mises quoted in *The Socialist Economy*, by Tom Bottomore, Hemel Hempstead, Harvester Wheatsheaf, 1990., p54.
11 *On the Economic Theory of Socialism*, by Lange, O and F M Taylor, New York, McGraw-Hill 1964.
12 Von Mises later presented this as a victory since his critics were forced to retreat to pseudo-market methods to come up with a system for a planned economy, although he still denied it would work, without being specific why (see, 'The Why of Human Action', *Plain Talk*, 1949, reprinted in: Ludwig von Mises, *Economic Freedom and Interventionism*, Indianapolis, Liberty Fund, 1990, p63).
14 For a fuller account of these issues, of which this is a summary, see *Marxist Economic Theory*, by Earnest Mandel, London, Merlin Books, 1968, pp634-7.
15 See *The Revolution Betrayed*, by Leon Trotsky, London, New Park Publications, 1973. Trotsky's classic account of the degeneration of the revolution is still essential reading today to understand what happened.

16 *The Destruction of Nature in the Soviet Union*, by Boris Komarov, London, Pluto Press, 1980.
17 These developments are detailed in *Industrial Innovation in the Soviet Union*, Edited by R Amann and J M Cooper, New Haven, Yale University Press, 1982, and in R P Dickenson, 'The Level of Research in Advanced Composite Materials in the Countries of the former Soviet Union', *Scientometrics*, 36 (1), 1996, p43-57.
18 Lionel Robbins, (1934), *The Great Depression*, London, Macmillan, p154.

Planning for the Planet: How Socialism Could Save the Enviroment

Chapter 7:
Summary and Conclusion - A warning to the Labour Movement

The Stern report concluded that cuts of 80% are needed in emissions to stabilise greenhouse gas levels. If decisive action is taken immediately to achieve this, in the next five to ten years, temperature rises could be limited to less than 2C and the worst effects of global warming avoided. It would therefore be wrong to bow to the idea, now promoted by climate deniers, that adapting to climate change is more important than mitigating its effects. It is true some global warming effects are already irreversible and will have to be dealt with. These should be manageable if effective action is taken soon and so do not justify abandoning attempts to stabilise emissions. Even if the situation becomes much more serious due to a lack of prompt action, it will still be necessary to cut greenhouse gases to achieve long term stabilisation, at the same time as adapting to climate effects.

As the dire consequences of global warming increasingly become clear, sections of big business and some in government, will look to geo-engineering measures as a low cost, easy way out of their dilemma. This possibility could result in outcomes that are nearly as bad as climate change itself and reinforces the need for urgent and effective action to reduce emissions.

The failures of the Durban and Copenhagen summits, meant to correct the failings of the Kyoto system, showed the inability of the capitalist class to tackle global warming. In advance, the UN had called the Copenhagen conference the last chance to avoid catastrophic global warming. In the event it just revealed the deeply antagonistic relations between the big powers preventing agreement on climate change. Even if the scheme proposed at Copenhagen had been implemented with the full support of the main players, including the USA and China, and with all the loopholes removed, cap-and-trade would still have been a flawed mechanism to prevent global temperatures from rising more than 2C. The scale of the cuts needed and the relatively short time available means that any method that relied on constructing market disincentives to pollute would be inadequate. At best, the impact of this approach would be gradual. It would reduce global emissions at far too slow a rate to meet the need identified by climate science to lower emissions 40% by 2020 - the cut required to keep temperature rises to below 2C.

Directly applied carbon taxes, as many Greens advocate, could have a bigger impact than cap-and-trade on greenhouse gas reductions. Leaving aside for the moment questions of fairness, there would still be limitations to the effectiveness of such a policy. Relying on the operation of price signals in this way, in a largely monopolised energy market, would have a relatively small impact. What carbon taxes would do though would be to hit the poorest sections of society, since the poor spend a greater proportion of their incomes on fuel. This would especially be the case if taxes were implemented on a scale intended to have a serious impact on emissions. Such regressive measures should be opposed by socialists.

Rather than backing the market-type system discussed at Copenhagen, many activists, seeing the urgency of the situation, are now calling for direct measures to be implemented to reduce greenhouse gases. These measures could include laws to establish a ceiling in emissions by a certain date, with any breach dealt with using criminal sanctions. However, if the world's ruling classes opposed the largely cosmetic measures proposed at Copenhagen any new approach with real teeth would meet with even more determined resistance. The evidence is now clear that despite their protestations to the contrary, governments in Britain and internationally do not intend to take any meaningful action to tackle climate change.

The financial and economic crisis that began in 2007 has made it likely that even token measures, like the Kyoto treaty, will be opposed by most states. For instance, the USA categorically refused to participate in an international treaty to reduce greenhouse gases, even when it was offered a system at Copenhagen that was full of loopholes. Environmental activists should join with the Labour Movement to fight the inaction of the capitalists. However, as well as campaigning for decisive action, political lessons must also be drawn from the 20 years that has been wasted by the capitalists in the battle against climate change.

Like most European governments, the USA is still supporting the 'lesser evil' of nuclear power as a way out of their dilemma. This is despite the evidence of the 2011 nuclear disaster in Japan and the very high long-term costs of nuclear power. These costs include storing ever increasing amounts of nuclear waste for tens of thousands of years, decommissioning power stations and creating a meaningful fund to deal with the effects of a future Chernobyl-type disaster. If true costs are considered, renewable energy sources, like wind, wave and solar power, become comparatively less expensive. However, the long-term costs of nuclear power will be effectively ignored by capitalist governments, so that the profits of the multinational firms that really control the political agenda will be affected to the minimum extent.

Only by eliminating the power of the big corporations can an alternative to the nightmare scenario of environmental disaster caused by a nuclear accident or global warming become a reality. Sustainable growth on a capitalist basis is not feasible, partly because the methods it can employ to achieve this are inadequate and flawed, but mainly because imperialist rivalry will prevent the international co-operation that is essential to make progress. The result is that the world will continue to hurtle headlong to disaster. The environment will still be treated as a 'free good' by the multinationals that dominate production and will be exploited at little cost to themselves.

The failure of market approaches to tackle climate change points to the need for a radical policy that addresses the root of the problem. This is the capitalist market system and the imperialist rivalry between nation states that it has spawned in the last hundred years. A change in the social system is the only way that will allow us to live in harmony with the natural environment into the foreseeable future. The premise for this must be the common ownership of the means of life, which will remove the antagonism between nation states that is threatening to destroy the planet, if it is applied internationally.

At one level, implementing the measures needed to address global warming is simple; no technological breakthrough is required. All that is called for is the wider adoption and further development of existing technology, such as wind, wave and solar power. In order to tackle climate change, many environmentalists think that big cuts in consumption are needed, requiring a fundamental change in lifestyle. They deny there is a 'technical fix' of simply switching over to alternative energy sources. It is true that there is no technical fix, but the decisive factor will be changing the social system, not cutting consumption. A social transformation will enable wind, wave and solar to be implemented, as well as a massive switch to public transport, without the need for reductions in consumption.

The key technical elements of an approach to reduce greenhouse gas emissions are:

- Rapid conversion to the use of renewable energy sources, such as wind, wave and solar power
- Big expansion of public transport
- Development of the rail network so that short and medium haul air travel can be reduced and then replaced
- Conversion of car industry to using renewable energy sources
- More research into renewable energy, such as clean coal technology, and using materials not based on oil products

In practical terms, to realise this programme will mean nationalising the main industries that dominate the economy. This will eventually need to be done throughout the world, encompassing the 147 multinational corporations that recent research has shown dominate the global economy. Since the operation of competitive markets degrades the environment, rejecting the market system is essential to tackle global warming. Doing this will require an alternative approach to organising production. Rational democratic planning is not just a viable alternative, it has huge inherent advantages over the market from the point of view of saving energy. For example, it could avoid the duplication of resources, planned obsolescence and wide-scale destruction and then rebuilding of factories, plant and machinery in the capitalist slump/boom cycle.

Nationalising (or renationalising) the energy and transport industries will, by removing the shackles of the market, lay the basis for a switch to renewables and for the massive expansion of public transport. The industrial sectors needing to be nationalised are the energy generating and distribution companies, vehicle manufacturers and bus and rail service providers. Another key aspect of the struggle to achieve a carbon neutral world will be to increase energy efficiency in the production of all manufactured goods and of housing. The need to reduce the intensity of energy use includes nearly all areas of the output of goods and services, so it will be essential to efficiently integrate the different sectors of the economy into an environmental plan. This in turn will require the public ownership of the 150 big corporations that presently dominate British society.

By taking no meaningful action for the past twenty years, the representatives of the capitalist market system have created a situation where some of the effects of global warming are irreversible. Regardless of future events, this is a historical indictment, in its consequences possibly ranking alongside capitalism's greatest crimes, such as the imperialist wars of the 20th Century.

To avoid the worst effects of climate change, decisive action needs to be taken now, but there is no sign of this happening due to the rivalries between the main industrial powers. This presents a grave warning to the international Labour Movement, that the task is urgent and it falls on our shoulders to implement a programme that can tackle climate change. The essential step to make this a reality is to replace capitalism with a democratic socialist system. The longer the delay, the worse will be the situation we inherit.

Since it poses the greatest threat to the planet, the primary focus here has been on climate change and ways to mitigate its effects. However, other dangers to the environment have been highlighted, which include those linked to nuclear power generation in particular. Threats also encompass non-nuclear toxic contamination, deforestation, unsustainable agricultural practices and species depletion. The book has attempted to show that two related factors underlie all these threats. They are the quest for profit by big corporations and at a more fundamental level, the inevitable tendency of competitive markets to degrade the environment.

For these reasons, the remedy of a democratic planned socialist society, put forward to combat the danger of climate change applies in addressing other environmental threats. The task is urgent. It must involve the political re-armament of the Labour Movement in Britain and internationally with a socialist programme. As a first step, this will require the creation of new parties to replace the discredited former workers' organisations, such as the Labour Party in Britain. These parties have totally failed over decades to implement programmes to reverse the degradation of the planet.

Planning for the Planet: How Socialism Could Save the Enviroment

Bibliography

Amalric, F, (1995) 'Population growth and the environmental crisis', in: Bhaskar, V. and A Glyn. (Eds). *The North, the South and the Environment*, London, Earthscan.

Amann R and J M Cooper, (Eds). (1982) *Industrial Innovation in the Soviet Union*, New Haven, Yale University Press.

Anon., (2009), 'One Million Climate Jobs Now!' A report by the Campaign Against Climate Change Trade Union Group for the Communication Workers Union, Public and Commercial Services Union, Rail, Maritime and Transport Union, Transport Salaried Staff Association and the University and College Union.

Baumol, W J, and T ten Raa, (2002), 'Wasily Leontief: In appreciation'. *Journal of Economic and Social Measurement*, 26, 1-10.

Bottomore, T (1990), *The Socialist Economy, theory and practice*, Hemel Hempstead, Harvester Wheatsheaf.

Clarke, D L, (1984), 'Planning and the Real Origins of Input-Output Analysis'. *Journal of Contemporary Asia*, 4 (4).

Coase, R A,(1960), 'The problem of Social Cost', *Journal of Law and Economics*, 1960, Vol 3, 1-44.

Cock, Martin and Bill Hopwood, (1996), *Global Warning. Socialism and the Environment*, London, Militant Publications.

Common, M and Sigrid Stagl (2005), *Ecological Economics. An Introduction*, Cambridge, Cambridge University Press.

Daly, H E, (1992), *Steady-State Economics*, London, Earthscan.

Dickenson P, (2003) *Planning Green Growth*, London, CWI Publications.

Dickenson, R P, (1996), 'The Level of Research in Advanced Composite Materials in the Countries of the former Soviet Union', *Scientometrics*, 36 (1), p43-57.

Ekins, P, (2000), *Economic growth and environmental sustainability, the prospects for green growth*, London, Routledge.

Engels, F, (1969), 'Letter to Lavrov', in Karl Marx and Frederick Engels, *Selected Works*, Vol. 3, Moscow, Progress Publishers.

Engels, F, (1969), 'Part Played by Nature in the Transition from Ape to Man', in: Karl Marx and Frederick Engels, *Selected Works*, Vol. 3, Moscow, Progress Publishers.

Fine, B and A Saad-Filho (2004) *Marx's Capital*, London, Pluto Press.

Fankhauser, S, (1993), 'Global Warming Economics: Issues and state of the art' CSERGE Working Paper GEC 93-28, CSERGE, University College London, London.

Georgescu-Roegen, N, (1986),'The entropy law and the economic process in retrospect' *Eastern Economic Journal*, Jan-Mar.

Glyn, A, (2006), *Capitalism Unleashed*, Oxford, OUP.

Hardt, Michael and Antonio Negri, (2000), *Empire*, Cambridge, MA, Harvard University Press.

Hussen, A, (2004), *Principles of Environmental Economics*, London, Routledge.

Jacobs, M (1999), 'Sustainability and Markets: on the neo-classical model of environmental economics', in *Planning Sustainability*, edited by Michael Kenny and James Meadowcroft, London, Routledge.

Kaliadina, S A, (2006), 'Leontief 'W W and the repressions of the 1920s: an interview', *Economic Systems Research* 18, (4) December.

Komarov, B, (1980) *The Destruction of Nature in the Soviet Union*, London, Pluto Press.

Kula, E, (1998), *History of Environmental Economic Thought*, London, Routledge.

Lange, O and F M Taylor, (1964), *On the Economic Theory of Socialism*, New York, McGraw-Hill

Lenin, V, (1925), 'The Tax in Kind', *Collected Works*, 1st English Edition, Moscow, Progress Publishers.

Lenin, V, (1970), *Imperialism –the Highest Stage of Capitalism*, Moscow, Progress Publishers.

Leontief, W, (1925), 'Balans naorodnovo khoziaistva SSSR-metodologicheskii razbor robotii TSSU'. *Planovoe Khoziaistva* (12), pp 254-258. (The balance of the economy of the USSR-a methodological critique of the work of the Central Soviet Statistical Directorate).

Leontief, W, (1941), *The Structure of the American Economy, 1919-1929*, Cambridge, Mass, Harvard University Press.

Leontief, W,(1986), *Input-Output Economics 2nd edition*, Oxford, Oxford University Press.

Luks F,(2010), 'Deconstructing economic interpretations of sustainable development: Limits, scarcity and abundance', in: L Mehta (Ed.), *The Limits to Scarcity*, London, Earthscan.

Mandel, E, (1968) *Marxist Economic Theory*, London, Merlin Books.

Marx, K, (1969), 'Letter to J B Schweitzer', in *Karl Marx and Frederick Engels, Selected Works*, Vol. 2, Moscow, Progress Publishers.
Marx, K, (1973), *Grundrisse*, Harmondsworth, Penguin Books.
Marx, K, (1976), *Capital, Vol. 1*, Harmondsworth, Penguin.
Marx, K, (1978), *Capital, Vol. 2*, Harmondsworth, Penguin.
Marx, K, (1981), *Capital, Vol. 3*, Harmondsworth, Penguin.
Meek R L, (Ed), (1953), *Marx and Engels on Malthus*, London, Lawrence and Wishart.
Meinshausen M, (2006) 'What does a 2C target mean for greenhouse gas concentrations? A brief analysis based on multi-gas emission pathways and several climate sensitivity uncertainty estimates', in H J Schellnhuber et al, (eds.) *Avoiding dangerous climate change*, Cambridge, Cambridge University Press,
Mises, L- von, (1936), *Socialism: An Economic and Sociological Analysis*, London, Jonathan Cape.
Mises, L- von, (1949), 'The Why of Human Action', Plain Talk, 1949, reprinted in: Ludwig von Mises, *Economic Freedom and Interventionism*, Indianapolis, Liberty Fund, 1990.
Pepper, D, (1993), *Eco-Socialism*, London, Routledge.
Perman R, Ma Y, McGilvray J and M Common, (2003), *Natural Resource and Environmental Economics*. Harlow, Pearson.
Rees, W, (1999), 'Scale, complexity and the conundrum of sustainability', in *Planning Sustainability*, edited by Michael Kenny and James Meadowcroft, London, Routledge.
Robbins, L, (1934), *The Great Depression*, London, Macmillan.
Sarkar, S, (1999), *Eco-socialism or eco-capitalism*, London, Zed Books.
Scott-Cato, M and M Kennett, (1999), *Green Economics*, Green Audit.
Stern, N (2007), '*The Economics of Climate Change, The Stern Review*', Cambridge University Press.
Sweezy, P, (1968), *The Theory of Capitalist Development*, New York, Monthly Review Press.
Trenberth, K E and Aiguo Dai (2007), 'Effects of Mount Pinatubo volcanic eruption on the hydrological cycle as an analog of geoengineering', *Geophysical Research Letters*, Vol. 34, L15702, doi:10.1029/2007GL030524.
Trotsky, L (1973), *The Revolution Betrayed*, London, New Park Publications.
Trotsky, L, (1975), 'Stalin as Theoretician', in *Writings of Leon Trotsky (1930)*, New York, Pathfinder Press.

Planning for the Planet: How Socialism Could Save the Enviroment

Index

Agriculture, greenhouse gas emissions from 79, 104-106
Amazon rainforest, destruction of 21
Arms spending, reduction of 83
Australian economy, input -output model 104-106

Bali summit, UN climate talks 57
Bangladesh, effects of climate change on 42
Bio-mass   103-104
Bolshevik government 127-128

Caesium 137,
  toxic radioactive element 14-15
Cambridge Centre for Climate Change Mitigation 22
Campaign against Climate Change 85, 86
Cap and trade, carbon emissions permit system 44-45, 67, 102
Capitalist system
  choice in 45-46,
  compulsion to accumulate in 122
  constraints on 46-59
  duplication of resources in 83-84
  'rules of the game' in 101
Car industry, green programme for 77-78
Carbon dioxide, emissions 57
by industrial sector 104-106
Carbon taxes, (also see eco-taxes) 67-68, 140
Cardis, E 16
CFC chemicals, *see* Ozone layer breakdown
Chernobyl nuclear disaster 10-12, 140
China
  greenhouse gas emissions   74
  nuclear building programme 16
  one child policy 121
  role in climate talks 52-53, 55-57
Choice under capitalism, *see* Capitalist system and Consumer choice
Clean Coal technology 74, 79-80
Climate change
  argument over adaptation to 30-32, 38-39
  deniers   9, 32-38, 139
  direct state intervention to tackle 68
  hockey stick controversy 36
  use of technology to tackle 38, 65-67, 79-80
'Climategate', University of East Anglia 33-34
Clinton, Bill 51
Cock, Martin 3
Command and control, in economic management 42, 53, 54
Commoner-Erlich equation 60, 70-72
Conspicuous consumption 119

Consumer
  behaviour 97
  choice 95-97
  committees 92, 96
  needs and preferences 92, 95
Contingent Valuation Methods 72
Copenhagen summit, UN climate talks 5, 41, 54-59, 68, 139-140
Cost Benefit Analysis 69-70
Cramer, W 28
Crawford-Browne, D 22
Czarist empire, in pre-revolutionary Russia 126-127

Daly, Hermann 59
Deepwater Horizon, oil spill accident 9, 18-19
Deforestation 9, 20, 59, 81, 142
Desertification 9, 79
Disraeli, Benjamin 46
Duplication of resources, see Capitalist system
Durban, UN climate talks 5, 41, 54, 68, 139

Earth Summit, UN climate talks, 1992 1
Eco-Marxists 121-122
Eco-socialism 121-123
Eco-taxes 45-46, 59
El Niño 27
Electric and hydrogen fuelled cars, see Car industry
Emanuel, Kerry 25
Energy intensity, need to reduce 81
Engels, Frederick 120, 122
Environmental Impact Coefficient, see Commoner Erlich equation
Environmental intensity 70, 119
Environmental Kuznets theory, see Kuznets theory
Expanded reproduction of capital, see Marx
Extreme weather events, link to global warming 23-25

EU, role in climate talks 56-58
European Union, see EU

Feedback effects, see Global warming, tipping point effects
Final demand, component in economic models 104, 109, 110,
First World War 127
Fisheries destruction 20, 21-22
Five-year plan, of 64 Labour Government 100
Flight of capital, see Green Keynesianism
Forest carbon credits 58-59
Fukushima nuclear disaster 5, 10, 13-16, 140

Gandhi, Indira 121
General Strike 64
Genetically modified organisms, see GMOs
Geo-engineering 30-32, 139
Global South 70-72, 119
Global warming
  controversy over extent of danger 37-38
  definition 25, 26-27
  extent human induced 23, 36-37
  extent irreversible 28-30
  tipping point effects 26-28
GMOs 19
Gorbachev, Mikael 133
Gore, Al 51
GOSPLAN 100
Great Depression 65
Green growth agenda 62
Green Keynesianism 63-65
Green programme for car industry, see Car industry
Greenhouse effect 25-26
Growth,
  bio-physical limits to 121, 123
  limits to, debate over 117-123, 141

Index

Gulf Stream 76

Hayek, F von 123, 125, 134-135
High-speed rail 65, 78-79
Himalayan glaciers, alleged disappearance of 34
Hockey stick controversy, *see* Climate change
Hopwood, Bill 3
Housing, energy saving in 85
Huhne, Chris 41
Hurricane Katrina 23, 24-25

Imperialism 47, 48-50, 80-81
Import controls 59, 65
Incentives to stop polluting, *see* Neo-classical economics
India, population control in 121
Industrial sectors' interdependencies 104-106, 110-114
Innovation, see Technology
Input-output coefficient table 111
Input-output theory 101-102, 103-104, 109-114
Input-output transaction table 109, 111
Institutionalist economic theory 66-67
Intergovernmental Panel on Climate Change, *see* IPCC
International Energy Agency 26
Iodine 131, toxic radioactive element 14-15
IPCC 28, 57, 58, 71
    relation to Climategate controversy 32-34

Katrina, see Hurricane Katrina
Kautsky, Karl 90
Kerry, John, US Senator, role in climate talks 56
Khruschev, Nikita 131-132
Krakatoa, volcanic eruption 30
Kulaks, *see* Soviet Union

Kuznets theory, related to environment 30
Kyoto Treaty 5, 41, 54-58, 68, 74, 140

Lange, Oscar 124-125, 134-135
Lenin, Vladimir 47, 48, 124, 127, 128
Leontief matrix 113
Leontief, Wassily 7, 97-99, 100
Leverman, A 28
Limits to Growth, see Growth
Locked-in theory, see eco-taxes
Lovelock, James 120
Low intensity agriculture 34-35
Low-hanging fruit, economic theory 66
Luxury expenditure, elimination of 83

Malthus, Thomas 120
Make the polluter pay principle 43-46, 54
Mandel, Ernest 130
Market failure theory, *see* Neo-classical economics
Market research 91, 92, 97
Market socialism 134-136
Market system, *see* Capitalist system
Marshall Plan 65
Marx, Karl
    on limits to growth 118
    on Malthus 120
    on socialism 89-90, 117
    theory of simple reproduction of capital 100, 107-108
    theory of expanded reproduction of capital 108
Masters, J 23
Minerals Management Service, US regulatory body 18
Mises, L von 92, 97, 105, 123, 124
Monbiot, George 5, 10, 16, 120
Montreal Protocol 20, 51-52
Mount Pinatubo, eruption of 31

151

Nation State, *see* Imperialism
National Academy of Sciences 74
National accounting and planning 98
National Centre for Atmospheric Research 31
Neo-classical economics, summary of, related to environment 43-44
Neoliberalism 42 *and passim*
Net present value 69-70
Neurath, Otto 91
New Labour government 67
New technology to tackle climate change, *see* Climate change
Nuclear power
 danger 10-17, 140
 plant, design flaws 15-16
 cost of 69-70, 140
Nuclear
 radiation, health effects 16-17
 fusion 38

O'Connor, James 121
Obama, Barak 55-56
Ocean warming 36-37
Offsetting arrangements, in climate talks 57-59
Offshore wind generation, *see* Renewable energy sources
Oil industry, *see* Deepwater Horizon
Operational research 91
Optimising energy use 104-105
Oreskes, Naomi 37
Ozone layer, breakdown of 9, 20

Permit trading, *see* cap and trade
Physiocrats 99
Planned economy, *see* Planning
Planned obsolescence 83

Planning
 capitalism, attempts at 99, 100-101
 the environment 102-106
 need for democracy in 81, 84, 91-93, 101, 103 117-118, 124-126,
 techniques 94-114
Plutonium, production linked to nuclear weapons 12
Population control 119-121
Post-modernism 34-35
Potsdam Institute of Climate Research 28
Prices of production, *see* Real prices of production
Productivity of labour 95
Property rights, economic theory 42-43
Public choice approach, *see* Property rights
Public ownership 80-81, 86, 141
Public transport, development of 76-80

Quality-of-life 119
Quesnay, Francois 99

Radioactive waste, *see* Nuclear power, danger
Rainforest, effect on of offsetting proposals in climate talks 58-59
Rational agent theory, *see* Neo-classical economics
Real prices of production 125, 134-135
Renewable energy sources 73-76, 140-141
Rivers Pollution Act, 1876 46
RMBK, boiling water nuclear reactor 11
Robbins, Lionel 125
Russian Revolution, 1917 91, 117, 123, 126
 degeneration 127-129

Sale of Food and Drugs Act, 1874 46
Science, public scepticism about 34-35
Scientists for Global Responsibility 34
Scripps Institute of Oceanography 36

Sea surface temperatures, *see* Hurricane Katrina
Second Law of Thermodynamics 123
Second World War, Keynesian measures in 63-65
Sectoral distribution of emissions, *see* Carbon dioxide
Seeding the atmosphere, *see* Geo-engineering
Shadow market value, *see* Neo-classical economics
Siege economy, *see* Green Keynesianism
Simple reproduction theory, *see* Marx
Singer, F 36
Slump/boom cycle 142
Social Darwinism 120
Socialist Calculation Debate 117, 123-126, 134-136
Soviet Union 7, 90, 119, 126-134
   bureaucratic ruling caste in 129
   collapse 130-134
   command economy 129-130
   destruction of environment in 118, 131-132
   planning in 92, 93, 129-130, 132-136
   role of kulaks in 129
Soviets 127
Species extinction 9, 20, 81, 142
Sponsorship bias, *see* Science
Stalin, Joseph 110, 123, 128-131
Stalinism 121, 123
Standard accounting conventions 100, 109-110
Standard industrial categories 102
Steady-state economy, critique 59-62
Stern report 26, 27 *and passim*
Stern, Nicholas, *see* Stern report
Stockholm International Peace Research Institute 83
Sustainability gap 94

Tableau Economique 108
Taylor, F 124-125, 134-135
Technology, *see* Climate change
Three Mile Island, nuclear accident at 11

Tipping points, *see* Global warming
Tobin tax, on financial speculation 59
Tokyo Electric Power Company 15
Toxic waste
   linked to nuclear power 10, 12
   linked to non-nuclear contamination 18-20, 81
Transformation problem 99
Transitional society 124
Trotsky, Leon 64, 110, 124, 127-129

Unemployment, elimination of 83, 94, 95
US National Institute of Health, *see* Nuclear Radiation, health effects
USA, role in climate talks 54-56, 68
USSR, see Soviet Union
Utopian socialists 89

Vestas, wind turbine manufacturer, strike at 63, 64

Wind, wave, solar power, *see* Renewable energy sources
Worker Co-op's 92
Working class, creative power of 84
WW2, *see* Second World War

153

Contacting the Socialist Party in England and Wales

Want to join the fightback?
Join the Socialists!

The relentless persuit of profit brought about the banking crisis and recession. Our world is run on that basis - the short sighted, chaotic capitalist system that exists only to enrich the fat cats.

We need an alternative. Taxing the rich, such as the bankers, and cancelling projects like Trident nuclear weapons would be a start. But more fundamental change is needed.

We need socialism! The banks and major industries would be publicly owned and democratically controlled.

It would mean democratic planning of the economy to meet the needs of all and to protect the environment.

The Socialist Party has a proud record of struggle and currently plays a leading role in the cmapaigns against the cuts, putting forward both a strategy for the fightback and a socialist alternative.

- If you agree with what you read in these articles from the Socialist - then you should join us!
- To locate a Socialist Party branch in your area text 07761818206 with your name and postcode
- Write to us at the Socialist Party, PO Box 24697, London E11 1YD
- Call our national office on 020 8988 8777
- Call our regional organisers:

East Mids: 0116 223 0534
London: 020 8988 8786
North East: 0191 421 6230
North West: 07769611320
South East: 07894 716 095
South West: 07759796478
Southern: 023 8057 5649
Wales: 02920440571
West Mids: 0247 655 5620
Yorkshire: 01142646551